Racial Disparities in the Department of the Air Force Military Justice System

SHAMENA ANWAR, JHACOVA WILLIAMS, NELSON LIM

Prepared for the Department of the Air Force
Approved for public release; distribution is unlimited.

PROJECT AIR FORCE

For more information on this publication, visit **www.rand.org/t/RRA1751-1**.

About RAND

RAND is a research organization that develops solutions to public policy challenges to help make communities throughout the world safer and more secure, healthier and more prosperous. RAND is nonprofit, nonpartisan, and committed to the public interest. To learn more about RAND, visit www.rand.org.

Research Integrity

Our mission to help improve policy and decisionmaking through research and analysis is enabled through our core values of quality and objectivity and our unwavering commitment to the highest level of integrity and ethical behavior. To help ensure our research and analysis are rigorous, objective, and nonpartisan, we subject our research publications to a robust and exacting quality-assurance process; avoid both the appearance and reality of financial and other conflicts of interest through staff training, project screening, and a policy of mandatory disclosure; and pursue transparency in our research engagements through our commitment to the open publication of our research findings and recommendations, disclosure of the source of funding of published research, and policies to ensure intellectual independence. For more information, visit www.rand.org/about/research-integrity.

RAND's publications do not necessarily reflect the opinions of its research clients and sponsors.

Published by the RAND Corporation, Santa Monica, Calif.
© 2024 RAND Corporation
RAND® is a registered trademark.

Library of Congress Cataloging-in-Publication Data is available for this publication.
ISBN: 978-1-9774-1193-8

Cover: Delanie Stafford/U.S. Air Force.

About This Report

Although the existence of racial disparities within the Department of the Air Force (DAF) military justice system has been well established, the causes of these disparities have not yet been determined. This has hindered the ability of the DAF to address these disparities through policy changes. This report uses a mixed methods approach to identify how disparities in the military justice system can arise, at what stages of the system the disparities occur, and what factors can explain the disparities.

RAND Project AIR FORCE

RAND Project AIR FORCE (PAF), a division of RAND, is the Department of the Air Force's (DAF's) federally funded research and development center for studies and analyses, supporting both the United States Air Force and the United States Space Force. PAF provides the DAF with independent analyses of policy alternatives affecting the development, employment, combat readiness, and support of current and future air, space, and cyber forces. Research is conducted in four programs: Strategy and Doctrine; Force Modernization and Employment; Resource Management; and Workforce, Development, and Health. The research reported here was prepared under contract FA7014-22-D-0001.

Additional information about PAF is available on our website: www.rand.org/paf/

Funding

Funding for this research was made possible by the independent research and development provisions.

Acknowledgments

We are extremely grateful to the Air Force personnel who participated in interviews and helped us better understand the military discipline system. We thank Rosanna Smart for providing information on marijuana legalization laws, Devon Hill for assistance with conducting interviews, Paul Emslie for setting up the initial dataset, and Melissa Bauman for editing a draft of the report. We are also indebted to Lisa Jaycox and Ray Conley, who provided project oversight and assisted with difficulties encountered along the way.

Our quality assurance reviewers were Brenda Moore of the University at Buffalo, SUNY, Jennie Wenger of RAND, and Jeremy Weber, a retired colonel in the Air Force. Each reviewer made invaluable contributions to the accuracy, clarity, and comprehensiveness of this report. We thank them for making the time to provide such perceptive reviews.

Summary

Issue

Although the existence of racial disparities within the military justice system has been well documented, the causes of these disparities have not been determined. Identifying the factors that are causing disparities is crucial to developing tailored policy options to reduce these disparities.

This study sought to answer the following questions within the context of the Department of the Air Force's (DAF's) military justice system:

- How might disparities within the DAF military justice system arise?
- How much of the racial disparity in Article 15s and court-martial referrals is explained by potential racial differences in offending rates and career fields in which the consequences of offending could be more dire?
- Are there further racial disparities among individuals issued an Article 15 or referred to a court-martial in terms of how their cases are adjudicated?

Approach

- We used information obtained from stakeholder interviews and policy reviews to develop process maps of the entire military discipline process, which yielded key insights into how racial disparities can arise.
- We merged detailed personnel data from the Air Force Personnel Center on all active-duty enlisted airmen in the DAF (fiscal years 2010 through 2019) with DAF discipline data from the Automated Military Justice Analysis and Management System (AMJAMS) to determine the extent to which racial differences in Article 15s and court-martial referral rates can be explained by career field, as well as an extensive set of personnel variables that can potentially proxy for offending behavior.

- We used AMJAMS data to determine whether, conditional on being issued an Article 15 or referred to a court-martial, there are racial disparities in the punishments airmen receive.

Key Findings

- Among enlisted male airmen rank E1–E4 (where discipline is most concentrated), Black airmen were 86 percent more likely to be issued an Article 15 or referred to a court-martial than White airmen.
- The disparities between White airmen and other race/ethnicity groups were markedly smaller: Article 15 and court-martial referrals were 27 percent more likely for American Indian/Alaska Native airmen, 8 percent more likely for Hispanic airmen, equally likely for Hawaiian Native/Pacific Islander airmen, and *less likely* for Asian airmen than White airmen.
- Conditional on being issued an Article 15 or referred to a court-martial, there are no further racial disparities against Black airmen in the punishments received. Black airmen referred to a court-martial are actually less likely to be convicted than White airmen and face lower sentences, conditional on conviction. Among airmen issued an Article 15, there are no racial differences in punishments received.
- About one-fifth of the Article 15 and court-martial referral disparity between Black and White airmen is explained by racial differences in career field and variables that might proxy for offending rates, including ZIP code characteristics of the airman's home of record and their Armed Forces Qualification Test scores. A key strength of this study is that we were able to rule out many of the factors that have long been considered probable causes of the racial disparity at this stage.
- The remaining four-fifths of the disparity in Article 15s and court-martial referrals is unexplained. Although definitive explanations are lacking, the results are consistent with a situation in which disparate treatment may be at least partly responsible for the disparity.
- Although the analyses presented here cannot definitively determine that disparate treatment is a cause of the disparity, any alternative reasoning put forward must explain why there are significant unex-

plained disparities in Article 15 and court-martial referral rates but Black airmen do better among those referred to a court-martial.

Policy Implications

- Collecting detailed data on administrative actions would allow for a more complete understanding of the nature and extent of racial disparities within the DAF's military justice system. Efforts to collect data on administrative actions are underway in the DAF, although the data are not currently collected in a centralized database that can be linked to other personnel and military discipline datasets.
- Having a diverse group of individuals make discipline decisions might mitigate disparities and increase trust in the process. This is especially true given that the analyses presented in this report indicate the biggest disparities occur in terms of who is issued an Article 15 or referred to a court-martial; at this stage of the system, there is a lone decisionmaker who, despite consulting with trusted advisers, ultimately wields a lot of discretion.
- Countermeasures to reduce individual biases within the discipline system should go beyond traditional trainings. In particular, these preventive measures should focus on making changes to the system such that the impacts of individual biases are mitigated.
- Evidence-based reforms are needed to ensure that the policies implemented are effective in reducing disparities in the DAF military justice system. Rigorous evaluation assessments of policy impacts should be conducted to ensure implemented policies are having the desired effect.

Contents

APPENDIXES

Figures and Tables

Figures

Tables

CHAPTER 1

Introduction

There is long-standing evidence that large racial disparities exist within the military justice system. A task report commissioned by the Department of Defense (DoD) in 1972 found that while Black service members composed 11.5 percent of the armed forces, they constituted 34.3 percent of those tried in a court-martial (DoD, 1972). About 50 years later, several studies have indicated that the size of these disparities has hardly changed (Robinson and Chen, 2020). Studies conducted by Protect Our Defenders (Christensen and Tsilker, 2017), the Government Accountability Office (GAO, 2019), and the Department of the Air Force (DAF) Inspector General (IG; DAF IG, 2020) have found that, over the past ten years, Black service members have been roughly twice as likely as White service members to face military discipline. This disparity is present across all services and is seen both in who is issued an Article 15 (a nonjudicial punishment) and in who faces a court-martial.

Although there has been a wealth of evidence documenting the existence of racial disparities within the military justice system, as of yet, the causes of these disparities have not been determined (Robinson and Chen, 2020). In particular, racial differences in who receives discipline can be caused by myriad factors, including (1) racial differences in offending rates, which can occur because of previous systemic inequities; (2) the concentration of certain racial groups in career fields that might punish a given infraction more harshly; and (3) disparate treatment, whereby Black and White service members who have similar characteristics and commit the same offense receive different punishments. Identifying the factors that are causing these disparities is crucial to developing tailored policy options to reduce these disparities.

Project Overview

In this study, we used a mixed methods approach to examine the causes of the racial disparity within the DAF military justice system. We merged detailed personnel data from the Air Force Personnel Center (AFPC) on all active-duty enlisted airmen in the DAF from fiscal years 2010 through 2019 with DAF discipline data from the Automated Military Justice Analysis and Management System (AMJAMS). The AMJAMS data provide information on which DAF airmen were issued an Article 15 or referred to a court-martial and details the offenses the airmen were charged with and the punishment received (if any). These discipline data allow us to examine disparities at two stages of the discipline process. The first stage identifies which airmen were either issued an Article 15 or referred to a court-martial. The second stage focuses on the punishments received among those who were issued an Article 15 or referred to a court-martial. These quantitative data are used, along with stakeholder interviews and policy reviews, to answer the following questions:

1. **How might racial disparities within the DAF military justice system arise?** We used information obtained from stakeholder interviews and policy reviews to develop process maps of the entire military discipline process, from the time an offense is alleged through the final adjudication of the offense. While prior studies provided an overview of the adjudication process for more-serious offenses, our process maps document the entire process. Furthermore, our maps note what information decisionmakers consider and the amount of discretion they have, which provides important insights into how racial disparities can arise.

2. **How much of the racial disparity in who is issued an Article 15 or referred to a court-martial is explained by potential racial differences in offending rates and career field?** This analysis uses the merged AFPC-AMJAMS data to determine the extent to which racial differences in Article 15s and court-martial referrals can be explained by an airman's career field and variables that might proxy for offending behavior, such as the characteristics of the ZIP code of their home of record, Armed Forces Qualification Test (AFQT)

scores, and whether they received a waiver for previous offending behavior. While some prior studies controlled for limited airmen characteristics, our study is, to our knowledge, the first to exploit the extremely detailed personnel information available in the AFPC data to try to explain the disparities in who is issued an Article 15 or referred to a court-martial.[1] The racial disparity that remains once these factors are controlled for could reflect disparate treatment or could reflect remaining racial differences that were not controlled for. Collectively, these analyses will provide more clarity on the relative roles of various factors in driving the racial disparity present at this stage of the process.

3. **Are there further racial disparities among individuals issued an Article 15 or referred to a court-martial in terms of how their cases are adjudicated?** The analyses presented here use the AMJAMS data to determine, conditional on being issued an Article 15 or referred to a court-martial, whether there are racial disparities in the punishments airmen receive.[2] To our knowledge, this analysis is the first to examine disparities in the full set of punishments individuals can receive and to control for the severity and type of offense they were charged with.[3] We combined the results found at this punishment stage with the results found at the first stage to provide a more complete picture of what is driving racial disparities throughout the military discipline process.

Throughout this report, unless otherwise noted, the term *racial disparity* (or *racial difference*) refers to the raw difference in a discipline outcome variable that occurs when no other variables are controlled for. We focus

---

[1] The GAO report (2019) controlled only for service member gender, education level, rank, and years of service.

[2] Although the AMJAMS data include details regarding the charged offense, the data do not include more-detailed information that is typically stored only in case files, including information about the nature of the offense (beyond offense type), facts of the case, and credibility of witnesses.

[3] The GAO report (2019) examined disparities only in court-martial outcomes (but did not examine Article 15 sentences) and did not account for detailed controls of the severity of the offense or of the adjudicatory pathway.

3

on explaining the racial disparity only among enlisted active-duty airmen within the DAF to keep the scope of the project more manageable and with the recognition that most of the discipline activity occurs among enlisted airmen rather than officers. When possible, our analyses focus on the disparities present among all race/ethnicity groups, although some of our more in-depth analyses and explanations focus on the disparity between Black and White airmen because the data indicate that the disparity present between these two groups is significantly larger than it is for any of the other groups.[4]

Structure of the Report

In Chapter 2, we provide a high-level overview for how the military discipline process works. In Chapter 3, we identify the size of the disparity in Article 15 issuances and court-martial referrals and examine what might explain the racial disparities that arise at this stage of the process. Chapter 4 focuses on the racial disparities present at the punishment stage. Finally, Chapter 5 presents the implications our results have for reducing racial disparities within the DAF's military justice system.

---

[4] The period examined in the report is 2010–2019, before the creation of the Space Force. For this reason, we refer to service members within the DAF as airmen, as opposed to airmen and guardians.

CHAPTER 2

Overview of the Military Discipline Process

In this chapter, we present a high-level overview of how alleged violations of the Uniform Code of Military Justice (UCMJ) are adjudicated for enlisted airmen and discuss the implications this process can have for racial disparity research on the military justice system. Appendix A provides a more detailed write-up of the process, including the purpose and jurisdiction of the military discipline system, an in-depth description of the various proceedings outlined here, the information that decisionmakers consider, and the potential effects that involvement in the system has on airmen.

The summary of the military discipline process presented here (and in Appendix A) is based on our review of various policy directives and scholarly articles, as well as patterns observed in the discipline data and the semistructured interviews we conducted with ten subject-matter experts.[1] These subject-matter experts were either serving or had served as a commander, staff judge advocate, defense attorney, or military judge in the DAF.[2]

---

[1] The policy directives consulted include Air Force Instruction (AFI) 36-2907 (on adverse administrative actions), AFI 51-202 (on nonjudicial punishments), AFI 51-201 (on the administration of military justice), and the Manual for Courts-Martial (DoD, 2019).

[2] In the interviews, we had subject-matter experts walk us through how cases progress through the system, focusing on who the decisionmakers are, what information they consider, and what their options are for adjudicating a case. Because the subject-matter experts we interviewed had experience with different parts of the military justice system, we asked them somewhat different questions. For example, when speaking with commanders, we asked about the initial handling and investigation of an alleged incident and discussed both the administrative action and the Article 15 process. Our

The Military Discipline Process

Figure 2.1 presents a high-level mapping of the military discipline process for any alleged violation of the articles listed in the UCMJ, no matter how minor or serious the offense may be. The authority that decides on the disciplinary action depends on how serious the offense is. Within the context of this report, a minor offense can be thought of as an offense that might occur in the context of an employer-employee relationship.[3] This often includes such violations as being late to work, not completing physical fitness sessions, not completing tasks as assigned, or having one's uniform out of

FIGURE 2.1

High-Level Process Map of the Military Discipline Process

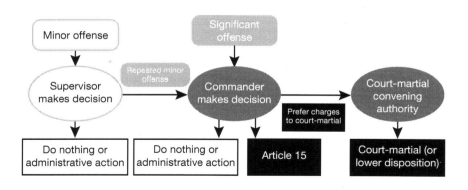

interviews with staff judge advocates, defense attorneys, and military judges focused more on the Article 15 and court-martial process.

[3] Throughout this report, our definition of a *minor offense* is different than it is defined in *The Military Commander and the Law* (Judge Advocate General's School, 2022), which defines a minor offense as typically being an offense for which the maximum punishment would not involve confinement for longer than one year. Throughout this report, we consider a minor offense to be an offense that can be handled by a supervisor, as opposed to a more significant offense that must be handled by the squadron commander.

regulation. These types of violations will generally be handled by the individual's direct supervisor, who is often a higher-ranked enlisted individual or a lower-ranked officer. A supervisor can either elect to take no action or issue an administrative action; an administrative action generally takes the form of a memo that records the wrongdoing of the individual. Administrative actions have various levels of severity, with a letter of reprimand being the most serious version. While these actions do not carry any explicit punishment, they can still have a serious negative impact on an airman's life, because these actions can affect their performance report and form the basis for more-serious action if the airman gets in trouble in the future.[4]

Offenses that are considered to be more significant are adjudicated, at least initially, by the squadron commander. A significant offense includes any offense that is considered serious—including anything that would be a civilian criminal offense (such as driving under the influence [DUI], a drug crime, or larceny)—as well as a repeated instance of a minor offense. For example, if an individual has been disciplined by their supervisor multiple times for being late, the next instance of lateness might be referred to the squadron commander for adjudication.

The squadron commander will determine whether an investigation is necessary. Depending on the type of offense, the case will be investigated by Security Forces, by the Office of Special Investigations, or through a Commander Directed Investigation.

The squadron commander may decide either to take no action or to issue an administrative action, similar to the disposition options available to a supervisor. However, the squadron commander also has the authority to initiate the Article 15 process, which is an adjudicative forum that (1) allows the commander to lay out the charges to the airman that the commander is

---

[4] Throughout this report, an *administrative action* refers specifically to verbal counseling, a record of individual counseling, a letter of counseling, a letter of admonishment, and a letter of reprimand. The DAF refers to the last three of these as *adverse administrative actions* (AFI 36-2907, 2020). Although there are other administrative decisions that can be made that also have important consequences for individuals— including demotion, denial of reenlistment, and involuntary administrative separation or discharge (Judge Advocate General's School, 2022)—our use of the term *administrative action* in this report is not referring to these decisions. Note that many of these decisions can be consequences of receiving the outcomes shown in Figure 2.1.

considering issuing an Article 15 for and (2) allows the airman to provide a response to the commander.[5] The commander will then decide whether they want to issue the Article 15 and, if so, what punishment to levy. An Article 15 is a nonjudicial punishment that can result in a rank reduction, forfeiture of pay, and/or extra duty. If the squadron commander decides the offense needs to be adjudicated through a court-martial, which has more-serious sentencing options, they can prefer charges to the court-martial convening authority, who is a senior commander in their chain of command. The squadron commander will receive advice from the Staff Judge Advocate (SJA) office (i.e., the local legal office) regarding appropriate upper and lower disposition limits for a given offense, but commanders are free to ignore these bounds. The involvement of the SJA office is intended to lend some consistency to the discipline process so that similar cases will be treated in the same way. Note that while the SJA does not have to be involved if the commander is issuing an administrative action, the SJA must be consulted if the commander wants to issue an Article 15 or prefer charges to a court-martial.

Once the charges are preferred to the convening authority, that commander can refer the charges to a court-martial, or they can elect to have the case adjudicated through a less serious disposition method (such as an Article 15).[6] There are three types of courts-martial, which handle cases of varying levels of severity:

1. A summary court-martial can only issue a maximum confinement sentence of 30 days.
2. A special court-martial can issue up to a one-year sentence.

---

[5] The decision to issue an administrative action is technically a process as well, as the issuing authority allows the airman to provide a written response, and the issuing authority can decide to withdraw, sustain, or reduce the action in response. Appendix A walks through these processes in more detail.

[6] The term *prefer* is distinct from *refer* in the court-martial process: While they both indicate handing off the charges to another process, they are relevant at different stages of the court-martial. When a squadron commander decides a court-martial should handle an offense, they will *prefer* the charges to the court-martial convening authority. Once probable cause for these charges has been determined, the convening authority will *refer* them to a court-martial.

3. A general court-martial can sentence an individual to the maximum penalty allowed under the UCMJ (DoD, 2019).

Special and general courts-martial are similar to civilian criminal trials in that there are prosecutors and defense attorneys trying the case, with a military judge overseeing the proceeding. The accused can elect to have either the military judge or a panel of Air Force members decide on their case. The court-martial convening authority then can approve this final verdict or, in cases involving less serious offenses, has the authority to downgrade it (Weaver, 2020).

Neither an Article 15 nor a summary court-martial conviction is considered a criminal conviction, and thus airmen who receive these outcomes will not have a criminal record. In contrast, a special court-martial conviction is considered the equivalent of a federal misdemeanor conviction, while a general court-martial conviction is the equivalent of a federal felony conviction (Breen and Johnson, 2018). While defense counsel is required to be provided only to airmen whose cases are adjudicated through a special or general court-martial, the DAF in practice makes defense counsel available to all airmen charged with an offense regardless of how minor the offense might be.

Although we have outlined how the process works generally, there are a few important caveats to note. First, there is no formal definition of what constitutes a *significant offense*. Squadron commanders will usually make known their definition of an offense that needs to be brought to them, but it is likely that this classification will vary across squadron commanders. Thus, in some squadrons, supervisors might deal with offenses that are dealt with by commanders in other squadrons. In addition, the wing commander at some bases might decide that certain offenses (e.g., DUIs) need to be handled by them. Second, there are certain types of cases that have a relatively defined process. For example, all sexual assault cases must be sent directly up to the wing commander and cannot be handled by the squadron commander. Drug cases are also treated in a more standardized way: Positive marijuana tests typically result in an Article 15 and an administrative separation, while other use of illegal drugs typically results in a court-martial (DAF IG, 2020). Finally, the severity of a given offense (and thus how the offense is handled) can also be determined by the career field an airman is in. For example, it was noted to us in interviews that being late or falling asleep on duty would be disciplined much more severely if the airman were in Security Forces than if they were in Force Support, in large part because the potential consequences of this behavior in the former are more dire.

How Racial Disparities Can Arise

The mapping of the discipline process indicates several ways that racial disparities can arise. First, there can be racial differences in offending behavior. Second, certain racial groups might be more likely to be concentrated in career fields where a given offense is punished more harshly. Third, decisionmakers can engage in disparate treatment, whereby an offense by a minority airman is disciplined more harshly than the same offense committed by a similar White airman. The process maps make clear that the key decisionmakers in the military justice process—supervisors, squadron commanders, and court-martial convening authorities—are all provided substantial discretion in how they adjudicate offenses. Aside from certain serious crimes that have a more defined process, as well as the handling of cases in a special or general court-martial, it is typically one decisionmaker who has full authority to decide on disciplinary action for an individual (although they typically will consult with trusted advisers before taking action).[7] Whenever decisionmakers are allowed to have discretion, it is possible for disparate treatment to occur (Quintanar, 2017; Goldin and Rouse, 2000).[8]

It is important to note that disparate treatment by decisionmakers can manifest in many ways. While it can reflect overt discrimination against minority racial groups, it can also reflect *implicit bias*, whereby decision-

---

[7] For example, a commander will need to consult with the SJA before issuing an Article 15. The commander will also often consult with the individual's supervisor and the first sergeant before making a decision. See Appendix A for more details.

[8] Although both Quintanar (2017) and Goldin and Rouse (2000) found evidence of disparate treatment by decisionmakers, those studies did not involve the military justice system.

makers engage in disparate treatment but are not conscious of it. An example of implicit bias might be decisionmakers having more empathy for airmen of the same race because they can identify with those airmen more and therefore being more likely to give them the benefit of the doubt. It is also possible that airmen may have a stronger bond with their supervisors or commanders when they are the same race and thus might be more likely to share mitigating circumstances related to their offense. Because the majority of supervisors and commanders are White, this will disadvantage minority airmen. Evidence of this form of disparate treatment was documented in the DAF IG report in which airmen stated that when individuals were late to work, White airmen were more likely to be asked if they were okay, whereas Black airmen would be disciplined (DAF IG, 2020).

Disparities that occur with a given incident can create further disparities in how future incidents are handled. Specifically, suppose minority and White airmen commit the same initial offense, but minority airmen are the only ones to receive an administrative action for that incident. If these airmen were to be charged with another incident, the minority airmen would likely receive more-serious disciplinary action than the White airmen because they already have a formal paper record, and the military justice system typically involves progressive discipline, whereby each successive incident results in more-serious punishment.

Data Availability and Implications for Research

The DAF only collects centralized data on offenses that are adjudicated through either an Article 15 or a court-martial. This means the first stage our analysis can examine—whether an airman is issued an Article 15 or is referred to a court-martial—is essentially at the midpoint of the process. Ideally, we would have liked to examine the disparities that occur at the administrative action stage, especially given that those we interviewed indicated the vast majority of offenses are handled at this lower level. Furthermore, interviews with airmen documented in the DAF IG report (2020) indicated that many Black airmen felt they were unfairly more likely to receive administrative actions, and supervisors noted that leadership pressured them to issue administrative action to Black airmen for very minor infractions. Having centralized data on administrative actions would have allowed our analyses to provide more context on the nature and extent of racial disparities throughout the entire discipline process. In particular, such data would have revealed whether White individuals were less likely overall to be charged with an offense or whether they were more likely to have a given offense adjudicated through an administrative action (rather than an Article 15 or court-martial).

CHAPTER 3

Racial Disparities in Article 15s and Court-Martial Referrals

We begin the analyses in this chapter by examining whether there were racial disparities in the rates at which enlisted airmen were issued an Article 15 or referred to a court-martial.[1] As noted in Chapter 2, this is the earliest part of the discipline process for which systematic data are collected by the DAF. After documenting that relatively large racial disparities exist, we conduct several analyses to investigate what might be causing this disparity. First, we examine the extent to which the overall disparity can be explained by racial differences in underlying characteristics, where the characteristics we include predict both the likelihood of offending and the likelihood of incurring disciplinary action conditional on offending. We then determine which of the many included airman characteristics actually explain the disparity. Note that, for simplicity, all analyses presented in this chapter combine the incidence of being issued an Article 15 or being referred to a court-martial into one outcome. In Appendix B, we show that our central conclusions would not change if we had instead looked at these two outcomes separately.

---

[1] Two reports published by the DAF IG and GAO used this same measure of the issuance of an Article 15 or being referred to a court-martial (DAF IG, 2020; GAO, 2019). Note that this measure is not actually picking up all cases that reach the Article 15 stage or higher, as we do not observe cases in which the Article 15 process is initiated but not completed, nor do we observe cases in which charges are preferred to a court-martial but then not referred. We expect those situations to be somewhat infrequent. As shown in Table 4.1, 90 percent of cases that make it to this stage are issued an Article 15, and 10 percent are referred to a court-martial.

To conduct the analyses in this chapter, we combined detailed person-nel data from the AFPC on all enlisted airmen with information from AMJAMS regarding whether those airmen were either issued an Article 15 or referred to a court-martial in a given fiscal year. For each fiscal year from 2010 through 2019, our analysis sample includes every enlisted airman who was on active duty that year. Individuals who served in multiple fiscal years during that period will have a separate observation for each fiscal year of service. This person–fiscal year data structure allows the characteristics of a given airman to change over time, which is especially relevant for some of the controls used, including location and prior disciplinary issues. The AMJAMS data are used to identify in which fiscal years (if any) these airmen were either issued an Article 15 or referred to a court-martial. The data are set up such that we are predicting whether an airman is issued an Article 15 or referred to a court-martial in a given fiscal year based on their characteristics at the end of the previous fiscal year. This necessitates dropping all individuals who are in their first fiscal year of service, as we would not have any personnel information on these individuals from the previous fiscal year. In total, we end up with approximately 2.5 million person-year observations, which corresponds to 470,330 unique airmen. Appendix B provides more detail on how the analysis dataset was constructed. All differences that are discussed throughout this report are statistically significant at the 10 percent level or better, unless otherwise noted.

Table 3.1 presents information on the race/ethnicity composition of the airmen in our starting analysis sample, where the defined categories are mutually exclusive.[2] To develop mutually exclusive categories that combine race and ethnicity, individuals are assigned to categories in the following priority: Hispanic, Black, American Indian/Alaska Native, Hawaiian Native/Pacific Islander, Asian, and White. We made the decision to combine race and ethnicity into one category, rather than keeping these as separate

---

[2] Among the sample used to construct Table 3.1, 87,131 airmen were classified as belonging to more than one of the five racial groups in the raw data. In Appendix B, we discuss how these airmen were classified into one race/ethnicity group. This classification resulted in 16,315 of these airmen being classified as Hispanic, 28,527 classified as Black, 12,940 classified as American Indian/Alaska Native, 13,830 classified as Hawaiian Native/Pacific Islander, and 15,519 classified as Asian. The central results in Chapters 3 and 4 are unchanged when these 87,131 mixed-race airmen are dropped.

TABLE 3.1

Race/Ethnicity Composition of Enlisted Airmen from Fiscal Years 2010 to 2019

Race/Ethnicity	Percentage
White	61.6
Black	17.0
Hispanic	15.0
Asian	3.5
Hawaiian Native/Pacific Islander	1.6
American Indian/Alaska Native	1.2

NOTE: This table is based on 2,452,169 person-year observations and includes all enlisted airmen.

categories, because that definition more closely resembles the race/ethnicity stratifications in previous literature (e.g., see GAO, 2019). Hispanic airmen thus include both White-Hispanic and Black-Hispanic airmen. We identified race/ethnicity using measures available in the AFPC data; this strategy identifies a larger fraction of Hispanic airmen than AMJAMS or the GAO report (2019) does. In Appendix D, we document the likely reason for this difference, but we note here that the race/ethnicity measures presented in Table 3.1 track closely with published estimates from the AFPC.[3]

Figure 3.1 examines whether there are racial disparities among airmen who are issued an Article 15 or referred to a court-martial in a given year. The results are presented per 1,000 airmen. For example, on average, 27.8 White airmen out of every 1,000 White airmen were either issued an Article 15 or referred to a court-martial in a given year from fiscal years 2010 through 2019. Because lower-ranked individuals tend to have more of these disciplinary incidents, we separated the results by lower and higher ranks.

The results among E1–E4 airmen indicate the largest racial disparity exists between Black and White airmen. The rates indicate that Black airmen are 71 percent more likely to be issued an Article 15 or referred to a court-martial than White airmen. These disparities between Black and White

---

[3]   AFPC published estimates indicate that 15.9 percent of active-duty airmen are Hispanic (as of June 2021).

FIGURE 3.1

Disparities in Article 15s and Court-Martial Referrals Among Enlisted Airmen, Stratified by Rank

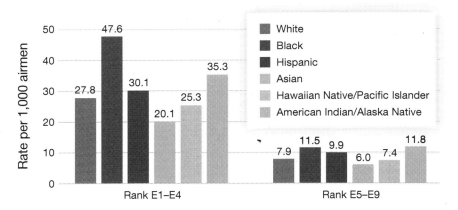

NOTE: The E1–E4 subsample includes 1,100,566 observations, and the E5–E9 subsample includes 1,351,577 observations. With the exception of the Hawaiian Native/Pacific Islander airmen, the discipline referral rates for each of the other race/ethnicities are statistically different from the discipline referral rate for White airmen at the 1 percent level.

airmen are in line with research by GAO (2019) and the DAF IG (2020).[4] We also find that the rates for American Indian/Alaska Native airmen are 27 percent higher than for White airmen, while the rates for Hispanic airmen are about 8 percent higher than for White airmen. Asian airmen are actually less likely to be issued an Article 15 or referred to a court-martial than White airmen, and there is no statistical difference between White and Hawaiian Native/Pacific Islander airmen.

---

[4] The actual discipline rate for a racial group is somewhat lower in our analysis than in the analyses presented in the DAF IG (2020) or GAO (2019) reports. This discrepancy occurs because both of those reports appear to collapse the data down to the airman level, so that a given airman has only one observation, and their discipline activity is coded as whether they had been issued an Article 15 or referred to a court-martial at least once during the multiple years considered. In contrast, our data are at the airman–fiscal year level. If the individual served for five years and was issued an Article 15 or referred to a court-martial only once, they would be coded as having five separate observations, with only one of the five observations coded as receiving disciplinary action. We prefer our measure because it identifies the rate per 1,000 who get into trouble in a given year.

Figure 3.2 examines how the racial disparities examined above differ across gender groups for airmen in ranks E1 through E4. The largest disparities occur among male airmen: Black male airmen were 86 percent more likely to be issued an Article 15 or referred for a court-martial than White male airmen.[5]

How Much of the Racial Disparity Can Be Explained?

As discussed in Chapter 2, racial disparities in the rates at which airmen are issued Article 15s or referred to a court-martial can occur for three main reasons: (1) racial differences in offending rates, (2) certain racial groups being more concentrated in occupations or bases where a given offense is punished more harshly because of the nature of their missions, and (3) disparate treatment. While we do not observe who is actually offending, the detailed personnel data provide many variables that can proxy for the likelihood of offending, which are described in more detail below. To better understand the relative role of these three factors in causing disparities, the analyses in this section examine the percentage of the observed racial disparity that can be explained by racial differences in base and occupation, as well as racial differences in variables that proxy for offending rates. In other words, we examine how much of the initial disparity is left once racial differences in these other variables have been controlled for. Because the results in the previous section indicated the largest racial disparities are found in the male E1–E4 subsample, this section will focus only on that subsample. In Appendix B, we present the results for similar analyses conducted on the other subsamples.

---

[5]   Hispanic airmen include White-Hispanic and Black-Hispanic airmen, as well as airmen of other racial groups; the racial/ethnicity groupings used here are similar to the groupings used in prior literature in this area (e.g., see GAO, 2019). However, for completeness, we stratified the results by race for Hispanic male airmen rank E1–E4 in Figure 3.2: The rate for White-Hispanic airmen is 31.8, whereas the rate for Black-Hispanic airmen is 50.7. This indicates that race is more strongly related to whether an individual is issued an Article 15 or referred to a court-martial than ethnicity is.

FIGURE 3.2

Disparities in Article 15s and Court-Martial Referrals, Stratified by Gender for Airmen Rank E1–E4

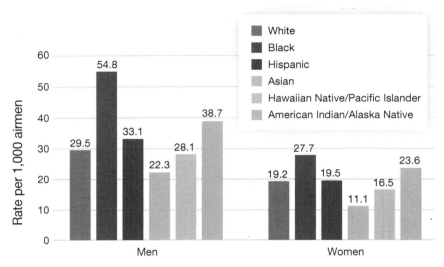

NOTE: All analyses were conducted on the rank E1–E4 subsample. The male subsample includes 888,879 observations, and the female subsample includes 211,687 observations. With the exception of Hawaiian Native/Pacific Islander airmen, all rate differences between White airmen and other airmen are statistically different at the 1 percent level for the male subsample. For women, the difference between Hispanic and White airmen is not significant, nor is the difference between Hawaiian Native/Pacific Islander and White airmen; the difference between White and American Indian/Alaska Native airmen is significant at the 10 percent level. The rates for Black and Asian airmen are statistically different from White airmen at the 1 percent level.

Table 3.2 presents the characteristics we included to proxy for offending rates.[6] To develop this list, we selected all variables in the personnel data for which prior research indicated an association with offending or for which our conversations with DAF personnel indicated the characteristic might be predictive of offending rates. The second column of Table 3.2 indicates how a given characteristic is measured. Each bullet point corresponds to a particular variable and presents the mutually exclusive values the variable can

---

6 Some of these variables may also reflect factors that are considered when deciding how to handle a given offense.

TABLE 3.2

Airmen Characteristics Being Used to Proxy for Offending Behavior

Characteristic	Options Included
Marital status	• Married, divorced, or single
Dependents	• Whether airman had dependents
Education level	• High school only, 1–2 years college, 3–4 years college, associate's degree, or bachelor's or post-bachelor's degree
AFQT percentile score	• Score of 1–49, 50–64, 65–92, or 93-plus
Home of record ZIP code characteristics	• For each of the following variables, we included four indicator variables that reflected which quartile of the distribution an individual fell in: – median income among ZIP code residents – percentage of Black residents in ZIP code – percentage of White residents in ZIP code – percentage of ZIP code residents who are high school graduates – percentage of ZIP code residents who are below the poverty line
Waivers	• Whether airman had a waiver for morals or drug and alcohol use
Training issues	• Instance of washback in technical training • AFSC reclassification or release from Guaranteed Training Enlistment Program
Prior trouble	• Previous referral EPR • Previous unfavorable information file • Previous control roster • Previous Article 15 • Previous court-martial
Rank	• E1, E2, E3, or E4
Years of service	• Indicator for years of service
Distance between base and home of record	• Less than 100 miles, 100–200 miles, more than 200 miles to 400 miles, more than 400 miles (but not overseas), or assigned to overseas location
State legality of marijuana	• Whether marijuana was legal in state where base was located

Table 3.2—Continued

Characteristic	Options Included
Population size of surrounding counties	• Less than 500,000 people, more than 500,000 people to 1 million people, more than 1 million people to 2 million people, or more than 2 million people

NOTE: AFSC = Air Force Specialty Code; EPR = Enlisted Performance Report. Appendix B documents the data source for each of these variables and provides more information on their construction.

take on. Several characteristics involve multiple bullet points, indicating that several distinct variables were included to measure that characteristic.

The potential links between many of the variables listed in Table 3.2 and offending rates are well known (e.g., see Lochner, 2020), so we focus our explanations here on some of the characteristics that may have a less obvious link to offending rates. For example, training difficulty was included because it is likely to reflect whether the airman has had trouble acclimating to the DAF, which could affect the likelihood of offending. ZIP code characteristics from the airman's home of record were included because the literature suggests that the environmental conditions in which children grow up (e.g., the poverty rate in their neighborhood) have a significant impact on a broad spectrum of future outcomes, including college attendance rates and earnings (Chetty, Hendren, and Katz, 2016), which in turn have been shown to have an important impact on offending behavior (Lochner and Moretti, 2004). Distance between the airman's base and their home of record was included because DAF personnel indicated that airmen might be more inclined to get into trouble if they continue to mix with their friends from home, as opposed to fully acclimating into Air Force culture. The state legality of marijuana in the airman's state of residence might affect the likelihood with which they engage in marijuana use, which is an offense in the military justice system and under federal law. Finally, airmen located in more populous areas might have more opportunities to get into trouble off base. It is important to note that some of these variables, such as whether the airman got into prior trouble, might reflect disparate treatment if disparate treatment is in fact one of the reasons why disparities in discipline outcomes occur. We consider this possibility in our interpretation of the results.

Figure 3.3 presents the results of our analyses, which examine how much the racial disparity in Article 15 and court-martial referral rates narrow when we control for the factors included in Table 3.2, along with AFSC, base, and fiscal year controls.[7] We control for these factors using a regression approach that is detailed in Appendix B. We do not present results for Asian and Hawaiian Native/Pacific Islander airmen because the results from the previous section indicated that these airmen are actually issued Article 15s and referred to courts-martial at an equal or lower rate than White airmen. Note that not all of the variables listed in Table 3.2 were available for all airmen: In particular, waiver status was available only for those who entered the DAF in 2010 or later, and state legality of marijuana and population size of surrounding counties was coded only for airmen assigned to a base within the United States. We thus do not include these three control variables in any of the analyses presented in this chapter, as it would require us to drop too much of our main sample. However, we conducted separate analyses (presented in Appendix B) within the smaller subsamples for which these variables could be measured and found these variables did not explain any of the disparity.

The height of each bar in Figure 3.3 represents the Article 15 and court-martial referral rate for each race/ethnicity group and represents the same rate presented in the male panel of Figure 3.2. For the bars representing Black, Hispanic and American Indian/Alaska Native airmen, the sum of the heights of the orange and gray sections indicates how much higher the rate is relative to White airmen, representing the total racial disparity between that racial/ethnic group and White airmen. The height of the orange section shows how much of that racial disparity is explained by racial differences in

---

[7]   Although we expect that one of the main reasons specialty might affect racial disparities is that some specialties will issue harsher punishments for a given offense, it is also possible that specialty may proxy for offending behavior if there is something unobservable about why airmen enter into a particular specialty that is predictive of being issued an Article 15 or referred to a court-martial. For example, extremist group members and gang members have joined or tried to join the military to learn tactics to use against rivals and law enforcement (National Gang Intelligence Center, 2015). Given that aim, it is reasonable that these individuals would be attracted to certain career fields, such as Security Forces, which might result in members of this career field having higher discipline rates.

FIGURE 3.3

How Much of the Racial Disparity in Article 15s and Court-Martial Referrals Is Unexplained Among Rank E1–E4 Male Airmen?

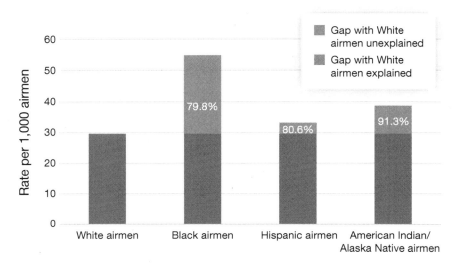

NOTE: Figure uses data on the male E1–E4 sample only. The unexplained gap represents the size of the racial disparity that remains once control variables that proxy for offending rates have been included, as well as controls for base, AFSC, and fiscal year. The exact specification used is detailed in Appendix B. The sample size is 888,879.

the variables controlled for. In other words, if Black and White airmen were similar with respect to all characteristics controlled for here, the Article 15 and court-martial referral rate for Black airmen (and thus the overall gap between Black and White airmen) would shrink by the height of the orange bar for Black airmen. The height of the gray section represents the portion of the disparity that is unexplained by any of the factors that we can control for: It is the disparity that remains once the above factors have been controlled for. The percentages listed for Black, Hispanic, and American Indian/Alaska Native airmen correspond to the percentage of the overall disparity that is unexplained.

Overall, the results in Figure 3.3 indicate that the majority of the disparities between White airmen and other racial/ethnic groups are unexplained by any of the factors that we can control for. Specifically, about four-fifths of the racial disparity between Black and White airmen is unexplained; the percentage of the disparity that is unexplained is also high for Hispanic and American Indian/Alaska Native airmen, although the raw disparity is smaller. Note that the results presented here focus on the collective explanatory power of the full set of included variables but do not parse which variables actually account for the majority of the explained disparity. This exercise will be conducted in the next section.

What Factors Explain the Racial Disparity?

The results in the previous section indicated that 20 percent of the disparity between Black and White airmen is explained by the collective set of variables controlled for in our analyses, but the results did not parse further which set of variables actually explains this 20 percent. It is easily possible that some of the included variables explain a large fraction of this 20 percent, while others explain almost nothing. For a given included variable to explain the observed disparity between Black and White airmen, it must be the case that there is a racial difference in the characteristic and that the characteristic is predictive of being issued an Article 15 or referred to a court-martial. For example, for AFQT scores to explain the disparity, it must be the case that Black airmen have lower average AFQT scores than White airmen *and* that those with lower scores tend to be more likely to be issued an Article 15 or referred to a court-martial.

The analyses in this section will seek to identify the variables that drive the explained disparity. Because the largest disparity exists between Black and White airmen, all analyses in this section focus only on these two racial groups (again restricting the sample to men in ranks E1–E4). From a policy perspective, identifying the set of variables that can explain some of this disparity can be just as important as identifying the role of disparate treatment, as the results will indicate whether the explained part of the disparity is primarily driven by racial differences in offending rates. The alternative would be that the explained part of the disparity is driven by certain racial groups being more concentrated in specialties or bases where a given offense is punished more harshly because of the nature of their missions.

The first two columns of Table 3.3 show how Black and White airmen differ with respect to the majority of the variables we included in our

23

TABLE 3.3

Predictor Variables' Relationship with Race and Article 15s and Court-Martial Referrals Among Rank E1–E4 Male Airmen

Variable	Percentage of White Airmen with Characteristic	Percentage of Black Airmen with Characteristic	Percentage of Those with Characteristic Either Issued Article 15 or Referred to Court-Martial
Marital status			
Married	35.3	28.1	2.5
Divorced	2.4	1.9	3.6
Single	62.3	70.0	3.9
Education level			
High school only	6.1	6.2	4.4
1–2 years college	72.1	75.3	3.9
3–4 years college, associate's/bachelor's/ post-bachelor's degree	21.8	18.4	1.7
AFQT score percentile			
1–49	8.4	17.8	5.0
50–64	26.1	38.9	4.0
65–92	54.8	40.3	3.1
93–99	10.8	3.0	2.0
Home of record ZIP code characteristics			
Black residents more than 15% of population	16.6	66.9	4.4
Black residents less than 15% of population	83.4	33.1	3.1
High school graduates more than 90% of population	53.3	39.7	3.2
High school graduates less than 90% of population	46.8	60.3	3.7

Table 3.3—Continued

Variable	Percentage of White Airmen with Characteristic	Percentage of Black Airmen with Characteristic	Percentage of Those with Characteristic Either Issued Article 15 or Referred to Court-Martial
Waivers			
Received a waiver for either morals or drug/ alcohol use	2.9	2.6	4.3
Did not receive a waiver	97.1	97.4	3.0
Training issues			
Training washback or AFSC reclassification	21.7	22.8	4.2
No training issues	78.3	77.3	3.3
Prior trouble			
Prior UIF, referral EPR, control roster, Article 15, or court-martial	8.0	10.3	4.9
No prior trouble	92.0	89.7	3.3
Distance between base and home of record			
Less than 100 miles	2.6	3.5	3.3
More than 100 miles (but base in United States)	81.9	78.6	3.4
Base overseas	15.5	17.9	3.9
Population size of surrounding counties			
Less than 500,000	30.2	30.4	3.8
More than 500,000 to 1 million	29.5	27.4	3.1
More than 1 million to 2 million	14.5	14.6	3.1
More than 2 million	25.8	27.7	3.3
Select Air Force Specialty Codes			
Maintenance	27.7	21.0	3.2
Security Forces	13.2	17.1	5.3

Table 3.3—Continued

Variable	Percentage of White Airmen with Characteristic	Percentage of Black Airmen with Characteristic	Percentage of Those with Characteristic Either Issued Article 15 or Referred to Court-Martial
Medical	3.7	6.2	3.6
Civil Engineering	8.1	7.5	3.2
Cyberspace Support	7.7	6.9	2.4
Munitions and Weapons	6.7	5.1	3.6
Intelligence	5.4	3.5	2.0
Force Support	2.0	7.2	5.0

NOTE: UIF = Unfavorable Information File. Sample uses Black and White male airmen who are rank E1–E4, which includes 545,375 White airmen and 136,263 Black airmen. Waivers, population size of surrounding counties, AFQT scores, ZIP code characteristics, and the distance between base and home of record are not identified for the full sample: The results in the table reflect percentages among the nonmissing for each of those variable categories.

analyses. For brevity, we do not show summary statistics for all variables, and for some variables we combine multiple variable options (shown in Table 3.2) into one option in Table 3.3 to more succinctly present the results. The third column of the table indicates the percentage of airmen (both Black and White) within that specific category who are issued an Article 15 or referred to a court-martial. For example, the results for AFQT score percentiles indicate that Black airmen receive lower scores than White airmen: In particular, 17.8 percent of Black airmen receive a score that is at the 49th percentile or below, compared with 8.4 percent of White airmen. The results from the third column indicate AFQT percentile scores are predictive of being issued an Article 15 or referred to a court-martial. While 5 percent of airmen with a score at the 49th percentile or below are issued an Article 15 or referred to a court-martial, only 2 percent of airmen with a score above the 93rd percentile are.

The results in Table 3.3 are helpful to understand which specific factors can explain some of the racial disparity at a more descriptive level. They indicate that such factors as AFQT scores, training issues, and prior trouble are likely to explain some of the disparity: All these variables are correlated with race and with discipline referrals. The results also indicate that such factors as waivers are unlikely to explain the racial disparity, because Black airmen are slightly less likely to have received a waiver. However, there are two shortcomings to this descriptive analysis:

1. While the results indicate which variables likely explain some of the racial disparity and which ones do not, they do not indicate the extent of the disparity each of these variables explains.
2. Many of the variables in Table 3.3 are correlated with each other, and thus some variables might seem more important than they are only because they are correlated with variables that are actually important.

We thus conduct a decomposition analysis below that more precisely identifies the extent to which each variable can explain the racial disparity.

Figure 3.4 presents the results from a Oaxaca-Blinder decomposition analysis. We provide details on this methodology in Appendix B. Each bar in the figure represents how much the racial disparity would narrow if Black and White airmen were similar with respect to that characteristic. This figure reveals the relative role each characteristic plays in explaining the overall disparity. Note that the decomposition analysis is identifying the impact of a given characteristic, holding constant the impacts of the other variables. Thus, even though we know AFQT score and occupation will be highly correlated, the estimates will tell us the explanatory power of AFQT score after accounting for occupation, and vice versa. We also included controls for whether the airman had dependents, their base, and the distance between their base and home of record. However, none of these controls explained a statistically significant amount of the racial disparity and therefore are not shown in Figure 3.4.[8]

---

[8] As was the case for Figure 3.3, we do not include controls for waiver status, state legality of marijuana, or population size because we do not observe these variables for a large fraction of our sample. In analyses presented in Appendix B, we show that these variables do not explain the observed racial disparity in Article 15s and court-martial referrals.

The sum of the percentages in Figure 3.4 is 23.0 percent, which is higher than the size of the explained portion in Figure 3.3 for Black airmen. This discrepancy occurs because controlling for certain variables actually widens the disparity; we do not show

FIGURE 3.4

What Specific Factors Explain the Disparity Between Black and White Rank E1–E4 Male Airmen in Article 15s and Court-Martial Referrals?

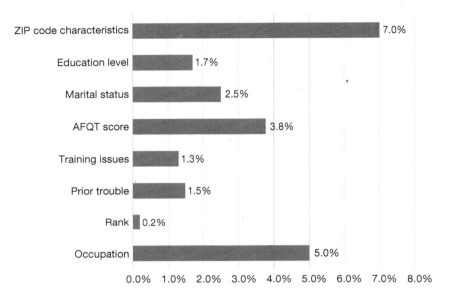

NOTE: Sample includes Black and White male airmen rank E1–E4, which consists of 681,638 observations. Results were obtained using Oaxaca-Blinder decompositions; details on the specification used are provided in Appendix B. With the exception of rank—which is significant at the 5 percent level—all variables presented in this table explain an amount of the disparity that is statistically significant at the 1 percent level.

The results in Figure 3.4 indicate that ZIP code characteristics from the airman's home of record, AFQT scores, and occupation play the biggest role by far in explaining the racial disparity between Black and White airmen in Article 15s and court-martial referrals. For example, if Black and White airmen came from ZIP codes that had similar characteristics, the racial dis-

these variables here for simplicity. Specifically, controlling for fiscal year widens the gap by several percentage points; when that is subtracted from the sum of the percentages from the explanatory variables here, one arrives back at the same overall explained amount.

parity would close by 7 percent.[9] With the exception of occupation, which explains 5 percent of the racial disparity, the other variables were included to proxy for the potential rate of offending. This implies that most of the *explained* part of the disparity is driven by potential racial differences in offending rates. However, these potential differences in offending do not reflect intrinsic racial differences but rather systemic inequalities. For example, previous discriminatory housing policies likely play a significant role in why Black airmen may grow up in worse environments than White airmen (Rothstein, 2017; as reflected in ZIP code characteristics), which can eventually make Black airmen more likely to offend. The role of occupation indicates that a smaller part of the explained gap is driven by Black airmen being more concentrated in occupations that are likely to punish a given offense more harshly. Finally, we noted earlier that the control for prior disciplinary issues might reflect disparate treatment, and thus we should be careful about the interpretation. However, the fact that this variable does not explain much of the racial disparity indicates that this issue should not be too much of a concern in this situation.

Discussion of Results

The results presented in this chapter indicate the presence of large differences between Black and White airmen in the likelihood of being issued an Article 15 or referred to a court-martial. Only about one-fifth of this disparity is explained by racial differences in career field and variables that proxy for offending rates. This one-fifth of the explained disparity is primarily driven by racial differences in variables that proxy for offending

---

[9] To the extent that airmen are a highly mobile population, in that they moved around a lot as they grew up, it is possible that the ZIP code characteristics of their home of record when they entered the DAF might differ from the characteristics of the area they mainly grew up in. Because this would essentially add random noise (because, for these individuals, ZIP code characteristics might not reveal anything), this could attenuate the importance of ZIP code characteristics. It is difficult to identify the size of this issue, however: Although about half of airmen have a parent in the military (Pew Research Center, 2011)—indicating they may be highly mobile during their youth—it is not clear what percentage of these airmen end up in a ZIP code right before they enter the DAF that is quite different from where they spent the majority of their time as children.

rates, including ZIP code characteristics of the airman's home of record and their AFQT scores.

While these results are useful in identifying what factors explain some of the racial disparity in who is issued an Article 15 or referred to a court-martial, they are just as useful in definitively identifying which factors do not explain the racial disparity. Our model includes many of the control variables that DAF personnel have long thought might explain these disparities, and our results indicate that the majority of these factors either have no explanatory power or have very little. For example, as noted earlier, one of the primary reasons that distance between home of record and current base was included was because DAF personnel felt that Black airmen tended to be based closer to home, which might result in them being more likely to offend. The fact that we find this factor does not explain any of the racial disparity in referral rates (and is thus not presented in Figure 3.4) is helpful to know, as it indicates that the DAF should not focus its attention on this issue in its efforts to address racial disparities going forward.

The results in this chapter indicate that the majority of the racial disparity in the issuance of an Article 15 or the referral to a court-martial is unexplained. This unexplained portion can represent disparate treatment, or it can reflect further racial differences in offending rates that were not properly controlled for with the proxy variables used. While we cannot guarantee that the characteristics included can perfectly proxy for offending rates, we controlled for an extremely rich set of characteristics. More specifically, even if there are other factors that affect Article 15 and court-martial referral rates outside the factors we controlled for, one would expect that many of these proposed factors are correlated with the variables controlled for. This implies that the percentage of the disparity that is explained might not increase substantially even if additional controls were accounted for, indicating that something besides racial differences in offending is likely driving at least some of the remaining four-fifths of this disparity. The analyses conducted in Chapter 4 will provide additional context regarding the unexplained disparity found at this stage, and we thus continue our discussion of what might be causing the unexplained disparity at the end of Chapter 4.

Racial Disparities in Sentences Received

The analyses in this chapter focus only on the set of individuals who were issued an Article 15 or referred to a court-martial and examine whether there were any further racial disparities in the sentences these individuals received. Specifically, for those issued an Article 15, a squadron commander can either decide not to issue any punishment or, in order of increasing severity, discipline the individual with a reprimand, extra duty, location restrictions, pay forfeiture, or a reduction in rank. Those referred to a court-martial can be acquitted on all charges. Those convicted in a court-martial can receive some of the same discipline options as an Article 15 but can also face much more severe punishments, including confinement and a punitive discharge. Because we intend for these analyses to complement the analyses conducted in Chapter 3, we restrict our analysis sample to enlisted White, Black, or Hispanic men.[1] The majority of the variables used in the analyses presented in this chapter were obtained from the AMJAMS data; see Appendix C for more details on the construction of the dataset.

---

[1] In this chapter, we do not examine outcomes for women or for Asian, Hawaiian Native/Pacific Islander, or American Indian/Alaska Native airmen. Because our analyses will further stratify the sample, the sample sizes become relatively small for these groups, which risks the possibility that these individuals could be identified. For our main sample of male White, Black, and Hispanic airmen, we include enlisted members of all ranks (E1–E9) rather than just the E1–E4 ranks considered earlier. This inclusion is primarily to increase the sample size. Chapter 3 indicated that the general patterns of racial disparities are similar across rank groups, although the disparities are largest among the lower ranks.

TABLE 4.1

Summary Statistics of Enlisted Male Airmen Issued an Article 15 or Referred to a Court-Martial

	Overall	White Airmen	Black Airmen	Hispanic Airmen
Airman characteristics				
White	57.3%	100.0%	0.0%	0.0%
Black	25.6%	0.0%	100.0%	0.0%
Hispanic	17.0%	0.0%	0.0%	100.0%
Age (years)	30.2	30.6	29.8	29.6
Rank E1–E4	76.4%	74.3%	79.3%	79.0%
Rank E5–E6	21.2%	23.0%	18.7%	19.3%
Rank E7–E9	2.3%	2.8%	2.0%	1.7%
Prior trouble				
Prior referral EPR	7.0%	7.2%	7.4%	6.0%
Prior UIF	15.0%	14.9%	16.2%	13.7%
Prior control roster	2.4%	2.5%	2.5%	2.2%
Prior Article 15	7.1%	6.8%	8.1%	6.6%
Prior court-martial	0.6%	0.6%	0.7%	0.6%
Maximum confinement for lead charge				
0 months to 1 year	59.3%	60.5%	56.7%	58.9%
1.5 years to 5 years	36.1%	35.0%	38.7%	36.1%
7 to 10 years	1.3%	1.3%	1.4%	1.6%
15 to 30 years	2.6%	2.7%	2.8%	3.0%
100 years	0.4%	0.4%	0.5%	0.5%
Offense type of lead charge				
Military	57.6%	59.2%	54.4%	56.8%
Property	6.4%	6.0%	7.6%	6.1%
Drug	13.7%	12.4%	16.6%	13.5%
Violent	6.0%	5.9%	6.4%	6.1%

Table 4.1—Continued

	Overall	White Airmen	Black Airmen	Hispanic Airmen
Society	12.8%	13.1%	11.6%	13.7%
Sexual assault	3.2%	3.1%	3.1%	3.7%
Weapons	0.3%	0.4%	0.4%	0.3%
Adjudication pathway				
Article 15	90.2%	90.2%	90.6%	89.6%
Court-martial	9.8%	9.8%	9.4%	10.4%
Observations	41,634	23,870	10,676	7,088

NOTE: Sample includes White, Black, and Hispanic male airmen who are rank E1–E9 and were either issued an Article 15 or referred to a court-martial.

Table 4.1 presents summary statistics on the main analysis sample used and describes the relevant information we observe on individuals at this stage that might affect the adjudication of their case. In addition to information on their demographics and previous career trouble encountered (which we described in Chapter 3), we also observe information on the offenses (or UCMJ article) an individual was referred for. Each offense has a maximum punishment listed in the UCMJ; we defined an individual's lead charge as the article that carried the highest maximum punishment. In Table 4.1, we describe the severity of the individual's lead offense according to the maximum period of confinement they can be sentenced to. We also identified the type of their lead offense, for which a military offense is any offense that would not be charged in the civilian criminal justice system; the two most common offenses charged within this category are willful dereliction of duty and making false official statements. Crimes against society primarily include drunken driving and drunken and/or disorderly conduct. The final two rows of the table show the percentage of individuals who had their case adjudicated with an Article 15 versus through a court-martial. We also observe the AFSC and the base where adjudication occurred but, for brevity, do not show these in the table. The first column presents the results for the full analysis sample, and the remaining columns show how these summary characteristics vary across race/ethnicity groups.

The results in Table 4.1 indicate there are minor differences in dominant offense characteristics across racial groups. For example, Black airmen are less likely than White and Hispanic airmen to be charged with a lead offense that carries a maximum punishment of one year or less: While 60.5 percent of White airmen have a lead offense that falls within this punishment range, only 56.7 percent of Black airmen do. There are also slight differences across offense types: Black airmen are less likely to be charged with a military crime than White airmen but are more likely to be charged with a drug offense.

The adjudication pathway rows in Table 4.1 indicate there are no racial differences in terms of who has their case disposed of through an Article 15 versus whose case is referred to a court-martial. Specifically, 9.8 percent of White airmen in this sample have their case adjudicated through a court-martial, while this percentage is 9.4 percent and 10.4 percent for Black and Hispanic airmen, respectively.

Racial Disparities in Article 15 Punishments

This section focuses on the set of airmen who were issued an Article 15 and examines the racial differences in the punishment they receive. Sixty-two percent of these airmen had all or part of their initial punishment suspended, meaning the suspended punishment does not go into effect unless the airman does not perform satisfactorily in the period after their punishment is issued. Because we wanted to examine differences in the punishment issued in terms of the airman's alleged infraction, as opposed to the additional punishment that was imposed if they did not behave satisfactorily postpunishment, we measure the punishment issued as the part of the initial sentence that is *not* suspended.

Figure 4.1 examines whether there are racial differences in who is issued the least severe punishments (receiving no punishment or receiving a reprimand only) and the most serious punishments (a pay forfeiture or a rank reduction). The figure presents a straight comparison of sentences across racial groups of airmen that is unadjusted for any covariates. In Table C.1, we present what the relevant racial comparisons in discipline outcomes would be if the following covariate characteristics were controlled for: all

FIGURE 4.1

Racial Disparities in Article 15 Punishments Among Enlisted Male Airmen

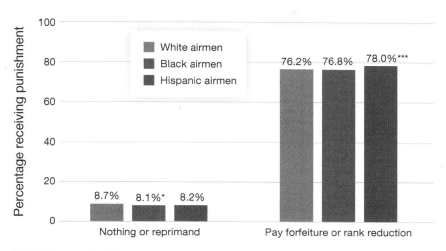

NOTE: The asterisks indicate that the percentage for Black and Hispanic airmen is significantly different than the percentage for White airmen at the 1 percent (***), 5 percent (**), or 10 percent (*) level. The sample includes White, Black, and Hispanic male airmen who are rank E1–E9 and were issued an Article 15 (*n* = 37,084).

characteristics listed in Table 4.1, along with the number of offense types the airman was charged with, their base and occupation, and the year the case was adjudicated. We conducted this alternative exercise because it is important to understand what the racial disparity is among airmen with similar characteristics and offense severity and type. However, the results in Table C.1 indicate the pattern of results does not appreciably change when covariates are included, and thus we present the unadjusted gaps for simplicity.

The results indicate there are no practical differences across racial groups in terms of the Article 15 sentences received. While 76.2 percent of White airmen issued an Article 15 are disciplined with either a pay forfeiture or a rank reduction (or both), the percentage is 76.8 percent and 78.0 percent for Black and Hispanic airmen, respectively. Thus, while Chapter 3 indicates there are clear racial differences in terms of the likelihood an airman will be issued an Article 15, there are no further racial differences in punishments received once airmen reach this stage.[2]

Racial Disparities in Court-Martial Outcomes

This section focuses on the sample of airmen who have their case referred to a court-martial for adjudication and examines the racial differences in sentences received. As described in Appendix A, the actual sentence an individual receives is the minimum of the adjudged sentence (what is handed down by the court-martial hearing officer, military judge, or panel) and the plea agreement in place (if any). We do not observe the actual sentence, so the results presented here are in terms of the adjudged sentence. While there is a possibility that racial disparities within the actual sentences might look different from disparities among the adjudged sentences, we think the adjudged sentence should provide a reasonably good measure with which to examine racial disparities present at this stage.

An airman's court-martial adjudicatory process can take many different paths; some paths are determined by the court-martial convening authority, and some are determined by the airman. More than half of individuals pled guilty to at least one charge.[3] Furthermore, there are three types of court-martial a case can be sent to, which have different sentencing capabilities, and there are several decisionmakers possible: hearing officers in a summary court-martial and a choice of a panel or military judge in a special or general court-martial. In this section, for simplicity, we examine racial differences only in final punishment outcomes and effectively ignore the possible adjudicatory paths. In Appendix C, we show that accounting for who has a plea agreement, which type of court-martial the case was tried in, and which decisionmaker determined the outcome does not change our general conclusions presented here.

---

[2] Figure 4.1 indicates that some of these differences are statistically significant, although the magnitude of the differences is quite small.

[3] A subset of the individuals who pled guilty executed a plea agreement with the convening authority. The data do not allow us to identify which individuals executed a plea agreement and which individuals pled guilty without a plea agreement.

As in the previous section, all figures presented in this section provide a straight comparison of outcomes across racial groups that does not control for any potential covariate differences. Table C.1 shows what these racial comparisons in court-martial outcomes are when individual and case covariates are controlled for.

Figure 4.2 indicates that 12.7 percent of White airmen referred to a court-martial were acquitted on all charges, while 18.2 percent of Black airmen were. Thus, Black airmen are significantly more likely to be acquitted on all charges than White airmen; Hispanic airmen also have an acquittal rate that is significantly higher than for White airmen.

The analyses in Figures 4.3 and 4.4 include only the set of individuals who were convicted in a court-martial and examine whether there were racial differences in the sentences received. Figure 4.3 indicates that Black and Hispanic airmen were about 4 percentage points less likely to be issued

FIGURE 4.2

Racial Disparities in Court-Martial Acquittal Rates Among Enlisted Male Airmen

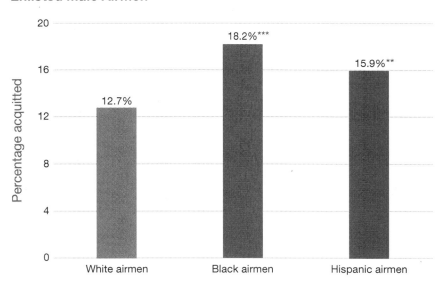

NOTE: The asterisks indicate that the percentage for Black and Hispanic airmen is significantly different from the percentage for White airmen at the 1 percent (***), 5 percent (**), or 10 percent (*) level. The sample includes White, Black, and Hispanic male airmen who are rank E1–E9 and were referred to a court-martial ($n = 4,058$).

FIGURE 4.3

Racial Disparities in Court-Martial Punishments Among Enlisted Male Airmen

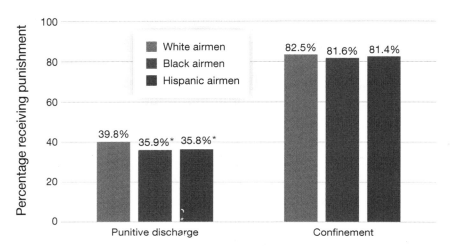

NOTE: The asterisks indicate that the percentage for Black and Hispanic airmen is significantly different from the percentage for White airmen at the 1 percent (***), 5 percent (**), or 10 percent (*) level. The sample includes White, Black, and Hispanic male airmen who are rank E1–E9 and were convicted in a court-martial ($n = 3,465$).

a punitive discharge than White airmen, although they were equally likely to be sentenced to confinement. Figure 4.4 presents racial differences in the average confinement sentences (in months); those who were not sentenced to confinement were included with an assigned sentence length of zero months. The results indicate that Black airmen are sentenced to significantly shorter periods of confinement than White airmen: While Black airmen have an average assigned sentence length of 6.9 months, the assigned sentence for White airmen is 10.3 months. Hispanic airmen are assigned to similar confinement lengths as White airmen.

The racial differences in outcomes at the court-martial stage indicate that, conditional on having a case referred to this stage, Black airmen have better outcomes than White airmen. Black airmen are significantly more likely to be acquitted on all charges than White airmen; among those who

FIGURE 4.4

Racial Disparities in Court-Martial Confinement Sentences Among Enlisted Male Airmen

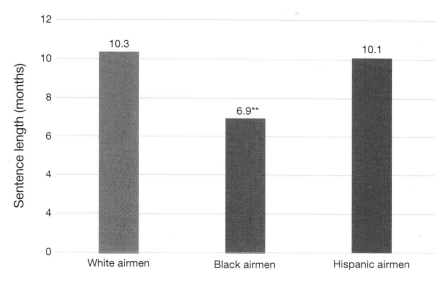

NOTE: The asterisks indicate that the percentage for Black and Hispanic airmen is significantly different from the percentage for White airmen at the 1 percent (***), 5 percent (**), or 10 percent (*) level. The sample includes White, Black, and Hispanic male airmen who are rank E1–E9 and were convicted in a court-martial (*n* = 3,465).

are convicted, Black airmen receive shorter sentences and are less likely to be punitively discharged.[4]

---

[4]   These results are broadly consistent with the patterns presented in the GAO report (2019), which indicated that Black airmen in the DAF were less likely to be convicted in a court-martial than White airmen and, conditional on being convicted, received a less severe sentence (although the results in the GAO report were not statistically significant). Our analyses in this chapter (as well as in Appendix C) expand on the specifications in the GAO report (2019) because we use more-detailed sentencing outcomes and show the general pattern of results presented here is robust to including detailed offense controls, as well as taking into account the adjudicatory pathway. The GAO report (2019) did not examine racial differences in Article 15 sentencing outcomes.

Discussion of Results

If we rule out the possibility that Black airmen are receiving favorable treatment in the court-martial process (i.e., that there is disparate treatment in favor of Black individuals),[5] one possible reason that Black airmen would do better than White airmen at the court-martial stage—consistent with the large unexplained disparity in Article 15 and court-martial referral rates found in Chapter 3—is that disparate treatment may be at least partially responsible for too many Black airmen being referred to a court-martial.[6] While probable cause is the evidentiary standard applied to refer an airman to a court-martial, a conviction requires that the airman's guilt be proved beyond a reasonable doubt. This is similar to the civilian criminal justice system. A grand jury that finds probable cause will return a true bill to bring an individual to trial. In our study of the DAF's military justice system, we note that, while disparate treatment can explain the pattern of results found here, the analyses presented here cannot definitively determine that disparate treatment is responsible for the unexplained disparity identified in Chapter 3, nor can they definitively conclude that the reason Black airmen do better at the court-martial stage is that a lower standard of evidence is being used to refer Black airmen cases relative to White airmen cases. In particular, it is possible that such factors as the degree of victim or witness cooperation, witness participation, and unwillingness to enter into a plea

---

[5]   Black airmen receiving disparate favorable treatment in the court-martial process did not seem likely, given the racial composition of decisionmakers and the fact that the potential for this behavior was not brought up in the DAF IG report (2020), which included surveys and interviews of airmen.

[6]   Because there is no way to objectively know whether a case should or should not go to a court-martial, we cannot distinguish whether these results occur because too many Black airmen are being sent to a court-martial or too few White airmen are being sent to a court-martial. The conclusions regarding disparate treatment are the same either way; for simplicity, we use the former terminology. The DAF has several checks in place—including probable cause determinations—to help ensure that only cases with sufficient evidence are referred to a court-martial.

While the results in Chapter 3 focus on the combined outcome of either being issued an Article 15 or being referred to a court-martial, we examine these outcomes separately in Appendix B and show that Black airmen are both more likely to be issued an Article 15 than White airmen and more likely to be referred to a court-martial.

agreement, among others, might explain why Black airmen have better outcomes at the court-martial stage. However, any reasoning put forward to explain the fact patterns found in Chapters 3 and 4 must explain why there are significant unexplained disparities in Article 15 and court-martial referral rates, but Black airmen do better among those referred to a court-martial. Put another way, if one were to claim that the disparities identified in Chapter 3 result from Black airmen being more likely to offend and/or committing more-serious offenses, then one would expect them to receive sentences that are at least as severe as White airmen at the court-martial stage, which they clearly do not.

Within the context of the above explanation, in which it is posited that disparate treatment might be partially responsible for the disparity in Article 15 and court-martial referral rates, it is important to consider why the court-martial process shows disparities in favor of Black airmen, whereas the Article 15 process shows no further disparities.[7] With the Article 15 process, the key individual responsible for deciding whether an Article 15 should be issued (typically, the squadron commander) is also the one determining the exact sentence. Thus, if there is disparate treatment in who is being issued an Article 15, this treatment would not be rectified in the Article 15 sentence issued. However, when cases are referred to a court-martial, the final decision is transferred to a separate process in a more structured setting that resembles civilian criminal case processing. While the convening authority retains certain powers over the direction of the case, there are many other decisionmakers involved, including trial prosecutors and defense attorneys, military judges, and court-martial panels of airmen. Because disparate treatment is more likely to exist in settings in which there are individual decisionmakers who yield considerable discretion, we might expect that disparate treatment would play a smaller role in the adjudication process of a court-martial, as it involves a more structured decisionmaking

---

[7] One distinction between the Article 15 and court-martial analyses presented in this chapter is that, with the Article 15 analysis, we examined only the punishment decision, whereas we examined both the decision to convict and the punishment decision (conditional on conviction) with the court-martial analysis. We cannot do a similar two-stage analysis of the Article 15 process because we observe only cases in which an Article 15 was issued and thus cannot examine the extent to which there are racial disparities in the decision to ultimately not issue an Article 15 that was initiated.

process. This is exactly what we find.[8] Many of the courts-martial in this study were decided by a group of panel members, which supports the notion that a group of decisionmakers is limited by group consensus, whereas an individual decisionmaker has greater latitude. It is important to note that, even if an airman is not found guilty, the process of being accused, investigated, and having their case adjudicated can still have a negative impact on the airman's reputation, career opportunities, well-being, and family.

---

[8] Although many courts-martial involve the military judge making the conviction and sentencing decision, this court-martial situation with a single decisionmaker is still different from the Article 15 process. Specifically, within the court-martial process, the military judge's decision is subject to more scrutiny, because it occurs within a trial framework and will be reviewed by the convening authority. In contrast, the full Article 15 process is handled by the commander and thus is not typically reviewed by a peer or more senior authority.

Even though Black airmen do better than White airmen at the court-martial stage, there still could be disparate treatment of Black airmen at this stage. In particular, if the strength of evidence or offense severity of the average Black airman is lower than that for the average White airman, it is possible that we could find that Black airmen actually do worse once these factors are controlled for (i.e., comparing the outcomes for equivalent Black and White cases). It is important to highlight here that a *disparity* refers to the difference in outcomes when no other factors are controlled for, whereas *disparate treatment* refers to the difference in outcomes when all relevant factors are controlled for. In Appendix C, we control for some offense severity characteristics and find that the outcome gap between Black and White airmen narrows. However, our analyses are not able to control for the strength of evidence. It is possible that the sign could flip (indicating disparate treatment of Black airmen) if we were able to control for strength of evidence.

CHAPTER 5

Conclusions and Policy Implications

Our analysis of disparities within the DAF military justice system revealed large differences across race/ethnicity groups. Among enlisted male airmen rank E1–E4 (for which discipline incidents are most common), Black airmen were 86 percent more likely to be issued an Article 15 or referred to a court-martial than White airmen. However, once making it to this stage, there were no further racial disparities against Black airmen in terms of the punishments received. The disparities between White airmen and other race/ethnicity groups were markedly smaller. American Indian/Alaska Native airmen were 27 percent more likely to be issued an Article 15 or be referred to a court-martial than White airmen, while Hispanic airmen were about 8 percent more likely. Asian airmen were less likely to be issued an Article 15 or referred to a court-martial than White airmen, and there is no statistical difference between White and Hawaiian Native/Pacific Islander airmen.

Further analysis on the Article 15 and court-martial referral disparity between Black and White airmen reveals that only about one-fifth of this disparity is explained by racial differences in career field and variables that proxy for offending rates. This one-fifth of the explained disparity is primarily driven by racial differences in variables that proxy for offending rates, including ZIP code characteristics of the airman's home of record and their AFQT scores. This implies that some of the large disparity at this stage is likely driven by racial differences in offending rates, which can arise because of the fact that systemic inequities have resulted in Black airmen being more likely to have certain characteristics that are associated with offending more often. These analyses are also helpful in that they can rule out several factors that have long been thought to contribute to racial disparities. In particular, our analyses show that such factors as education level, training issues, enlistment waivers, the state legality of marijuana, and the distance between an airman's base and home of record do not explain much of the disparity at all.[1]

The remaining four-fifths of the Article 15 and court-martial referral disparity between Black and White airmen is unexplained by any of the factors that we controlled for. This unexplained portion could be driven by disparate treatment, or it could occur because there were further differences among racial groups that affect Article 15 and court-martial referral rates that our controls did not account for. While it is important to stress that none of the analyses presented here can definitively determine whether disparate treatment is responsible for the disparity in Article 15 and court-martial referral rates, our key findings are consistent with disparate treatment potentially being at least partly responsible. First, although there definitely can be other factors that affect Article 15 and court-martial referral rates aside from the factors we controlled for, one would expect that many of these proposed factors are correlated with the variables we controlled for. This indicates that even if we were able to control for these additional variables, we would be unlikely to explain much more of the disparity than we are able to explain with our current set of variables. Second, the results found at the court-martial stage—whereby Black airmen are less likely to be convicted and face lower sentences conditional on conviction—could occur if a lower standard of evidence was potentially being used to refer Black airmen to courts-martial than was being used to refer White airmen. Determining this would require a case-by-case review of the evidence used to make the referral decision and witness participation, which is beyond the scope of the data used in this study. Without substantive analysis and review of the information presented to the commander in cases involving White and Black airmen, one cannot suggest a lower standard of evidence was potentially used to refer Black airmen to courts-martial. However, as we cannot explain why so many Black airmen have their case sent to a court-martial in the first place, it is possible that disparate treatment could be causing some of the initial disparity in the court-martial referral process. While none of

---

[1]   Each of these listed factors explains 2 percent or less of the racial disparity in Article 15 and court-martial referral rates.

the analyses presented here can definitively determine that disparate treatment is occurring, any alternative reasoning put forward regarding what is causing the large unexplained disparity in Article 15 and court-martial referral rates must explain why Black airmen have better outcomes than White airmen at the court-martial stage.

The quantitative results from this study should not be examined in a vacuum but rather should be examined alongside the qualitative analysis conducted by the DAF IG (2020). That survey of DAF airmen indicated that 36 percent of enlisted Black airmen, 54 percent of Black officers, and 73 percent of Black general officers felt disparate treatment existed within the military discipline system (DAF IG, 2020). An even higher percentage of these same respondents felt that Black service members were less likely to receive the benefit of the doubt in the discipline process (DAF IG, 2020). These qualitative findings from the DAF IG report are thus consistent with a scenario in which disparate treatment is at least partially responsible for disparities within the DAF military justice system.

Finally, it is important to note that the racial disparities observed here are not confined to the DAF military justice system. Studies by Christensen and Tsilker (2017) and GAO (2019) used a similar methodology to examine disparities across all military services and found racial disparities present in the Army, Navy, and Marine Corps justice systems, as well as the DAF justice system. Furthermore, significant disparities have long been documented in the civilian criminal justice system (Alexander, 2010; Sabol, Johnson, and Caccavale, 2019; Sentencing Project, 2018; Spohn, 2015). The civilian criminal justice statistic most directly comparable to the measure of Article 15 and court-martial referrals examined here is the arrest rate: The data indicate that Black individuals in the United States are arrested at a rate that is estimated to be five to nine times higher than the rate at which White individuals are arrested (Thomas, Kelly, and Simpson, 2020; Redbird and Albrecht, 2020). Thus, the racial disparities present in the DAF military justice system are not unique to this setting but rather are reflective of a widespread problem.

Policy Implications

This study has several implications for policy, as follows.

Collecting detailed data on administrative actions would allow for a more complete understanding of the nature and extent of racial disparities within the DAF's military justice system. As of this writing, the DAF collects centralized data only on offenses that reach the Article 15 stage or higher, although our interviews with airmen indicated that the majority of offenses are adjudicated through administrative actions. Having detailed data on administrative actions would provide a better understanding of how widespread disparities are within the system: i.e., do disparities exist only in Article 15s and referrals to courts-martial, or are there significant disparities in who receives an administrative action as well? Furthermore, these data would allow a greater understanding of what is driving disparities in Article 15s and court-martial referrals, because such data would provide a more complete picture of all the alleged offenses being committed. This would make it easier to disentangle whether Black and White airmen seem to be committing similar offenses but are sent to different adjudicative processes (e.g., an administrative action versus an Article 15) or whether Black airmen are more likely to be charged with more-serious offenses (and thus are more likely than White airmen to have their charge adjudicated through an Article 15 or court-martial).

Efforts to collect data on administrative actions are underway in the DAF, although not enough resources are available to collect these data in a centralized manner. However, the DAF has standardized the data that each base should collect, which includes the rank, age, gender, race, and ethnicity of both the issuer and the recipient, as well as the type of administrative action issued, the underlying offenses, and the number of prior administrative actions received by the recipient (Judge Advocate General's School, 2022). To fully capitalize on the information that administrative action data can provide, it is important to ensure that these data can be linked to current AFPC and AMJAMS data, so more-detailed information on the individual receiving discipline is readily available.

Having discipline decisions made by a diverse group of individuals might mitigate disparities and increase trust in the process. The analyses presented in this report indicate the biggest disparities occur at the Article 15 and court-martial referral stage, where an individual (typically, the squadron commander) will, while consulting with trusted advisers, ultimately be the lone decisionmaker who decides on the action taken. While the data did not identify any specific examples of disparate treatment by a commander, one might hypothesize that, if disparate treatment is a problem, it is less likely to occur when a team is involved in making a decision, as opposed to just one person, as it might be more difficult to engage in this behavior in a group setting. Evidence suggesting this possibility was borne out in the results, which indicated that Black airmen had better outcomes than White airmen at the court-martial stage (for which there is often a team of decisionmakers). Thus, one potential way to mitigate disparities might be to shift the decisionmaking authority at the Article 15 and court-martial referral stage from an individual to a group. For example, instead of having the squadron commander be the only decisionmaker involved, Article 15s and the preferral of charges to a court-martial could be determined by a diverse panel of decisionmakers, or the squadron commander's decision could be subject to a peer review process. These processes should operate outside the squadron commander's chain of command, and peer reviewers could remain anonymous; this would help avoid a situation in which these alternative decisionmakers feel pressure to simply go along with what the squadron commander would have wanted anyway. Given that the DAF IG (2020) report indicated that a significant fraction of Black airmen do not feel the discipline system is fair, moving to a process like this could also increase airmen's trust in the process.

Countermeasures to reduce individual biases within the discipline system should go beyond traditional trainings. While we noted above that one way to mitigate any potential biases would be to change who the decisionmakers are in the system, another option would be to make changes to the system the decisionmaker operates in, such that the impacts of whatever personal biases they may have are mitigated. Although having airmen in positions of authority attend bias training has been suggested (e.g., see DAF IG, 2020), there is no evidence that this type of training affects behavior (Worden et al., 2020; Forscher et al., 2019). An alternative way that could mitigate the biases of individuals would be to identify a default discipline option for a given offense, such that if a decisionmaker wanted to assign a different punishment than this option, they would need to document the reasons why. The principles of choice architecture indicate that individuals in this situation will typically choose the default option (Benartzi, Peleg, and Thaler, 2013), and thus an individual's personal biases are less likely to play a role in the final decision. Importantly, this choice setup still allows decisionmakers to retain discretion, which our conversations with airmen indicated was essential.

Another potential way to reduce the impact of decisionmaker biases would be to provide each decisionmaker (and their supervisor) with a summary of their discipline statistics and allow them to see how they compare with their peers. Decisionmakers who are identified as outliers in terms of their Article 15 and court-martial preferral rates of minority airmen might be motivated to rethink how they are making discipline decisions.

Evidence-based reforms are needed to ensure that the policies implemented are effective in reducing disparities in the DAF military justice system. While the results identified in this report indicate certain avenues to pursue when trying to reduce disparities, it is not certain that these policies will work. Because the underlying factors shaping disparities are complex, it will naturally be difficult to identify specific policies to reduce them. It is thus important to experiment with policies that should, in theory, be helpful based on what is known about the factors that might be causing disparities (such as the policies suggested above), then conduct rigorous evaluation assessments of their impacts to ensure the policies are having the desired effect. Policies that are successful in reducing disparities could then be scaled up.

The Military Discipline Process

This appendix presents a more detailed description of the DAF's military justice process than was discussed in Chapter 2. This process summary is based on the same sources that were noted in Chapter 2: specifically, policy directives, scholarly articles, our discipline data analysis, and our interviews with subject-matter experts. One of the reasons we present these process maps in such detail is that, to our knowledge, these are the first descriptions that provide sufficient detail on the entire process. In particular, while several previous articles have summarized the court-martial process (e.g., Jeanne M. Holm Center, 2015; Roan and Buxton, 2002; and Judge Advocate General's School, 2022), we have not seen a detailed summary of how administrative actions and Article 15s are administered in practice. We thus intend this to serve as a useful resource to those who want to understand the entire DAF military discipline process, including who the key decisionmakers are, what decisions they are making, what information on airmen they consider, and what the impacts of those decisions are on airmen. Although the discipline process for officers generally is very similar to the process for enlisted individuals, there are a few differences between these systems. The processes outlined below reflect the policies for enlisted individuals, as this group is the main focus of this report.

Background

Offenses Handled

The military justice system handles a wide variety of offenses, which can differ greatly in their severity. All activities considered a crime under civilian law will also be a crime under the military justice system. However, the

UCMJ also includes several offenses that are violations only of military law. Examples of the types of military offenses commonly adjudicated include failure to go (e.g., being late to work), making a false official statement (e.g., lying to your superior), dereliction of duty, and failure to obey a lawful order.

Why Is a Separate Justice System Necessary?

The preamble of the Manual for Courts-Martial states, "The purpose of military law is to promote justice, to assist in maintaining good order and discipline in the armed forces, to promote efficiency and effectiveness in the military establishment, and thereby to strengthen the national security of the United States" (Department of Defense, 2019, p. I-1). To fulfill this purpose, it is necessary for the military to have a justice system that is separate from the civilian one. First, as detailed above, there are certain actions that are considered to be an offense only under military law, and thus a separate justice system is necessary to adjudicate these offenses (Jeanne M. Holm Center, 2015). Second, because the consequences of many of the offenses listed in the UCMJ are well understood only by those in the military, it is necessary to have these offenses adjudicated by those in the military (Jeanne M. Holm Center, 2015). Third, active-duty members are stationed across the world; thus, many offenses take place outside U.S. soil. Because the military justice system has worldwide jurisdiction (unlike the U.S. federal courts), it can adjudicate all offenses committed by active-duty members, regardless of where those offenses occurred (Jeanne M. Holm Center, 2015). In fact, the original purpose of the military justice system was to ensure commanders could manage troops during war and on the battlefield (Dunlap, 2013).

Jurisdiction

All active-duty military members are under the jurisdiction of the UCMJ (DoD, 2019). However, there are instances when a crime committed might also fall under the jurisdiction of the state, such as when a criminal offense is committed off a military base. Because the military has worldwide jurisdiction for service members who commit an offense under the UCMJ, the legal office may request jurisdiction from civilian authorities; if jurisdiction is transferred, the legal office may take disciplinary action against the service member.

Does the Military Justice System Differ Across the Armed Services?

The core tenets of the military justice system are laid out in the UCMJ. Because every active-duty member of the DAF, Army, Navy, Marine Corps, and Coast Guard is subject to the UCMJ (GAO, 2019), all armed services are subject to the same military justice process. Specifically, the punishable offenses are the same, the decisionmakers are the same, and the disciplinary options are the same. However, each service is responsible for implementing the system, and thus there can be differences in practice across the services that still adhere to the rules outlined in the UCMJ. For example, while the UCMJ requires that defense counsel be provided to any airman facing a special or general court-martial, the DAF goes beyond this provision in that it also provides defense counsel to airmen encountering administrative actions and Article 15s. Furthermore, as outlined in detail in the GAO report (2019), each service records information on incidents in a different data system, and services differ in terms of the completeness of the data they collect. Specifically, as of 2019, only the Marine Corps and the DAF were collecting complete data on Article 15s. As a result, the ability to conduct in-depth analysis on racial disparities will differ across the services.

Key Participants in the Discipline Process

Commanders and Supervisors

Figure 2.1 and the corresponding discussion in Chapter 2 highlighted the key decisionmakers in the discipline process: supervisors, squadron commanders, and court-martial convening authorities. Supervisors have the authority to issue administrative actions, squadron commanders can issue either administrative actions or Article 15s, and convening authorities (either a wing commander or an even more senior commander) have authority to issue any of those lower disciplinary actions, as well as refer a case to a court-martial.

Staff Judge Advocate

The SJA runs the legal office at a base, which covers civil law, claims, and military justice (Jeanne M. Holm Center, 2015). The SJA represents the DAF; the office is part of the wing staff and reports to the wing commander. Within the SJA office, the Chief of Military Justice commonly works with squadron commanders at the base to provide advice on how a given discipline situation should be handled. Although these individuals can prosecute court-martial cases, usually such prosecution is done by circuit trial counsel (described below). Generally, the SJA office does not get involved in administrative actions handled at the supervisor level and typically is only called in when a case is adjudicated by a squadron commander or above.

Area Defense Counsel

The Area Defense Counsel (ADC) office provides advice and representation to airmen accused of UCMJ violations. Because the office handles only issues related to military justice, it is considerably smaller than the SJA office. There are about 75 ADC offices total: There is one office at most bases, although some bases share an ADC office with another base. Each ADC office usually has one captain and one paralegal, although bases that tend to have a lot of discipline incidents will have more staff. For cases handled at the administrative action level, the captain of the ADC office will provide legal advice to any accused member who seeks its services, regardless of whether it is a supervisor or a squadron commander who is issuing the action. When cases are handled at the Article 15 or court-martial level, the individual is automatically referred to the ADC office for legal advice. While the captain might assist in representing an individual in a court-martial case, circuit defense counsel (described below) usually will be the lead attorney. Unlike the SJA office, the ADC office does not report to the wing commander but rather to circuit defense counsel within the Trial Defense Division (Department of the Air Force Judge Advocate General, 2017). This arrangement serves to keep the ADC's actions independent from the SJA's actions.

Circuit Trial Counsel, Circuit Defense Counsel, and Military Judges

Circuit Trial Counsel and Circuit Defense Counsel serve as the prosecutors and the defense attorneys, respectively, for the majority of cases that are adjudicated through either a special or general court-martial, and these trials are overseen by military judges (Department of the Air Force Judge Advocate General, 2017). All three of these positions require significant litigation experience before one can serve at this level. These individuals are stationed across the world and typically will need to travel to handle a court-martial case in their jurisdiction.

Adjudication Process for Minor Offenses

In this report, *minor offenses* refers to offenses that are adjudicated by the individual's supervisor. As noted in Chapter 2, these often are such violations as being late, not completing physical fitness sessions, not completing tasks as assigned, or having one's uniform out of regulation. Our conversations with subject-matter experts indicated that the majority of offenses committed fall into this category. Generally, supervisors will have direct knowledge of the alleged violation (i.e., it happened in front of them), and thus additional investigations are not usually conducted at this stage. It would also be rare for supervisors to seek assistance from the SJA office regarding how to handle these minor violations.

When a supervisor is handling an alleged violation, they have the authority to either do nothing or issue an administrative action. These administrative actions can take on various forms, which are shown in order of increasing severity in Figure A.1. Verbal counseling is the least serious form of administrative action and is the only version that is not documented on paper (AFI 36-2907, 2020). An RIC needs to be documented on AF Form 174; the form can be used to record a verbal counseling session or can be used as written counseling (AFI 36-2907, 2020). The airman accused of the violation will need to sign the form to indicate they acknowledge the counseling. The remaining forms of administrative actions—Letters of Counseling (LOCs), Letters of Admonishment (LOAs), and Letters of Reprimand (LORs)—become increasingly serious, although all take a similar format, which is shown in Table A.1 (AFI 36-2907, 2020).

FIGURE A.1

Forms of Administrative Actions

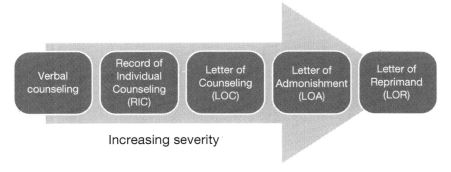

Increasing severity

TABLE A.1

Process by Which Administrative Action Is Issued

Step	Process
Step 1	Issuing authority drafts and delivers to airman a memo, which notes • whether the action is an LOC, LOA, or LOR • the alleged violation • the improvement expected.
Step 2	Airman can either • provide a written response • waive right to respond.
Step 3	Issuing authority • considers airman's response (if any) • makes final decision on whether to withdraw, sustain, or reduce administrative action.
Step 4	Airman acknowledges receipt of final decision.

Supervisors are supposed to handle the situation at the lowest discipline level possible because administrative actions are "intended to correct rather than punish behavior" (Judge Advocate General's School, 2016, p. 30; AFI 36-2907, 2020). For example, if an airman is late for the first time, this would typically not warrant an LOR but rather an action on the lower end, such as an RIC or LOC. However, if the airman has committed this offense multiple times, this new incident might warrant an LOR. Generally, when determining which action to issue, supervisors will consider the airman's discipline history and the context of the offense. The latter will not only include information about why the airman might have committed that violation but also will include the impact of the offense. In this way, an airman who is part of the Security Forces and is late may be punished more harshly than an airman who works in Force Support and is late. It was noted in our interviews that each unit has its own culture in terms of what type of behavior is considered unacceptable. Supervisors may also consult the first sergeant when they are determining what type of action to issue, especially if they want the first sergeant to be aware of ongoing disciplinary issues or if the supervisor thinks there might be a need for additional mentorship or guidance.

Administrative actions that are issued by supervisors can be filed in the airman's Personnel Information File (PIF), although our conversations with subject-matter experts indicated that these actions often were not formally filed anywhere.[1] Administrative actions that are not formally filed are often referred to as *desk-drawer actions*, because the supervisor will keep a copy of the action in their own filing system, but it will not be filed in any central way that will allow others to see the action. In contrast, if the supervisor elects to file the action in the PIF, it will generally be visible when performance reports are written or promotion decisions are made. These actions are often removed from the PIF at the end of the performance report cycle. There is no central filing system within the DAF that keeps track of administrative actions issued.

The extent to which squadron commanders are aware of these lower-level actions depends on the squadron. In some squadrons, the first sergeant will keep tabs on the administrative actions handed out by supervisors and will brief the commander on the overall picture. In others, the commander might note that they want to be briefed on all actions that reach the LOR level. In still other squadrons, squadron commanders may not know anything about these incidents unless an airman repeatedly receives administrative actions, and the situation is moved up to the squadron commander for adjudication.

---

[1] Unit commanders are no longer required to keep a PIF on each airman under their command, although PIFs can be kept at the squadron level if the squadron commander elects to use this system (Air Force Personnel Center News Service, 2008).

Role of Defense Counsel

As noted in Step 2 of Table A.1, airmen are provided an opportunity to respond in writing to their supervisor. Airmen can request assistance from the ADC office when drafting this response. Unlike with more-serious dispositional routes, for which ADC assistance is automatically provided (such as an Article 15), the ADC will not know about the potential administrative action in this case unless the airman reaches out to them. The likelihood of the airman reaching out will depend on whether the supervisor or the first sergeant suggests to the airman that they should see the ADC. If the airman requests assistance, the ADC will discuss the case with them and provide advisement on what should be included in the response to their supervisor. The airman will then draft their response, and the ADC will review and edit it. In some situations, the ADC may take the lead on writing the response.

Impacts on Airmen

There is no explicit punishment associated with an administrative action, as it mainly serves to document a wrongdoing. However, these actions will likely still have some negative impacts on the airman, including affecting their performance report and making them less likely to be recommended for training or leadership opportunities. These actions can also form the basis for more-serious action if the airman continues to get in trouble in the future. Generally, though, it was noted in our interviews that if an airman receives a few administrative actions at this level, but such actions never move up to a situation in which the squadron commander is asked to get involved, the airman should be able to continue on a successful career path. As noted in the policy directive on administrative actions (AFI 36-2907, 2020), these actions are intended to be corrective and not punitive, so they are not meant to have a long-term impact on an airman's career if such an action is just a one-time minor infraction.

Adjudication Process for Significant Offenses Not Adjudicated Through a Court-Martial

In this report, we define a *significant offense* as anything that has to be handled by a squadron commander or above. While the exact set of offenses included here will somewhat depend on the nature of the squadron and what the squadron commander has requested to handle, these offenses will almost always include any violation that is commonly thought of as a criminal offense (such as theft, DUIs, drug offenses, and assault), as well as any serious military offense (such as willful dereliction of duty and making false official statements). Another version of a significant offense is when the latest incident from an airman might be considered minor in isolation but represents a recurring problem (such as frequently being late). Because the tools available to supervisors do not seem to be able to correct the airman's behavior, this incident will be referred to the squadron commander, who has more options to discipline the individual. As shown in Figure 2.1, these cases can be adjudicated by the squadron commander, whereby the most serious disciplinary action they can take is to issue an Article 15, or the case can be preferred to the court-martial process. In this section, for simplicity, we discuss the process when the squadron commander makes the final decision, which necessarily means the final dispositional method will be an administrative action or an Article 15 (or nothing). In the next section, we discuss in detail the process whereby cases are preferred to a court-martial. Figure A.2 presents a flow chart that highlights the key events that occur once the squadron commander is informed of the incident. Below, we discuss each of these stages in more detail.

Initial Actions

Once squadron commanders are informed of an alleged offense in their squadron, they will usually collect initial information on the incident and then decide whether to launch a formal investigation. Investigations can be conducted in a few key ways. For criminal offenses, either Security Forces or the Office of Special Investigations will typically conduct the investigation. Security Forces often handles such offenses as a DUI or theft on base, whereas the Office of Special Investigations handles more-serious offenses,

FIGURE A.2

Flow Chart of Squadron Commander Decision

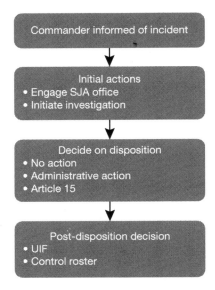

such as robberies and sexual assaults. Noncriminal offenses typically are investigated through a Commander Directed Investigation, whereby the squadron commander will have a senior noncommissioned officer, or an officer either within or outside the squadron, investigate the situation. Some of the offenses for which Commander Directed Investigations are used include harassment or creating a hostile work environment, as well as loss or misplacement of expensive equipment.

The other key action that squadron commanders take after being informed of an offense is reaching out to the SJA office for legal advice. The SJA office will provide advice regarding the investigation that should be conducted and appropriate upper and lower disposition limits for how to handle the offense once the investigation is completed. These bounds are determined by legal standards and by how similar incidents have been handled at the base. Squadron commanders are free to ignore these bounds, although several commanders noted that, typically, they try to stay within the bounds or else risk raising the attention of the wing commander, who may suspect that they are either overly lenient or overly harsh with regard to how they handle discipline. However, within these bounds, there is often a lot of leeway in how to handle a given offense.

Disposition Decision

Once the investigation has been conducted, the squadron commander will need to decide what disciplinary action they want to initiate. In this section, we focus on disciplinary situations whereby the squadron commander makes the final decision, which means the biggest decision they will make is whether the case deserves no action, an administrative action, or an Article 15. The process whereby an administrative action is issued was discussed in detail in the previous section. In Table A.2, we outline the process of how Article 15s are issued (Department of the Air Force Form 3070, undated; AFI 51-202, 2015).

The process described in Table A.2 highlights two areas within the Article 15 process for which airmen need to make important decisions. First, airmen have the right to reject an Article 15 and demand trial by court-martial. In practice, this is rarely done because the court-martial process can result in a much more serious outcome than an Article 15: The process is relatively long, punishments can be much heavier, and a conviction

TABLE A.2

Process by Which an Article 15 Is Issued

Step	Process
Step 1	Issuing authority uses DAF Form 3070, which notes • an Article 15 is being considered • which UCMJ articles were violated • investigation results or statements that will be used as evidence.
Step 2	Airman's response must note • whether they demand trial by court-martial instead of an Article 15 • whether they are requesting a personal appearance before the commander • their written response to the charges or potential punishment (if any).
Step 3	Issuing authority • considers the information the airman presented (if any) • makes final decision on whether to issue Article 15 and what punishment to impose.

can count as a federal criminal conviction. Furthermore, it was noted in our interviews that sometimes when a court-martial is requested, several charges will be added, making it even more difficult to refute the charges. For these reasons, the ADC generally recommends taking the Article 15 option when possible.

Airmen facing an Article 15 also need to decide whether they want to request a personal appearance before the squadron commander. The nature of these appearances can vary a lot depending on the command, but generally the commander will offer some perspective on their decisionmaking, and the airman will be given an opportunity to talk. Airmen are free to have defense counsel present at the appearance, and the squadron commander will often have the first sergeant present. Typically, a representative from the SJA office is not present, although this is up to the commander. It was noted in our interviews that personal appearances can be riskier than including a written response, so defense counsel most of the time do not recommend requesting a personal appearance, although it depends on how they expect the service member to present.

When determining which dispositional route to take, squadron commanders typically will consider the SJA's input, the individual's previous violations and performance reports, and the nature and context of the offense. As noted earlier in this appendix in the discussion of supervisor decisions, the culture of the unit can also determine how harshly a given violation is disciplined. There are also certain situations in which the squadron commander essentially does not have much discretion. For example, with marijuana offenses, the standard practice is to issue an Article 15 and then move to administratively separate the airman from the DAF (DAF IG, 2020).

If the squadron commander decides to issue an Article 15, they will also need to decide on what punishment to impose. Punishment options include a reprimand, extra duty, location restrictions, pay forfeitures, and a rank reduction. Commanders can select multiple options. All Article 15s issued are reviewed for legal sufficiency by the SJA and are entered into the AMJAMS database.

Post-Disposition Decisions

Once the squadron commander has decided on the dispositional outlet, they will need to determine whether the action should be placed in a UIF and whether the individual should be placed on a Control Roster (AFI 36-2907, 2020). Note that these decisions are not relevant when supervisors make the decision because they do not have the authority to take these actions.

If a record of the disciplinary action is placed in a UIF, this record will need to be reviewed whenever the individual is considered for promotion, reenlistment, permanent change of station, retraining, reclassification, and the Personnel Reliability Program (AFI 36-2907, 2020). In effect, placing this information in a UIF is a way to ensure that it is considered when important future decisions are made about the individual's career. If the action is not placed in a UIF, then only certain individuals might be aware of it.

Commanders can place individuals on a Control Roster if they want to restrict an individual's movements for a certain observation period (typically, six months). An individual on a Control Roster is ineligible for reenlistment, promotion, or permanent change of station reassignment (Jeanne M. Holm Center, 2015). While the UIF makes it unlikely these events will occur, putting an individual on the Control Roster ensures these events will not occur.

Our conversations with subject-matter experts indicated that generally these options are only considered once the disposition is at least at the level of an LOR. In terms of the way these actions are used, they tend to be added on to increase the impact of the LOR. For example, the following shows how these can be used in combination with an LOR with increasing severity:

- issue LOR by itself
- issue LOR and place LOR in a UIF
- issue LOR, place LOR in a UIF, and place airman on a Control Roster.

If an airman is issued an Article 15, it is almost automatic that the Article 15 will be placed in a UIF and the airman will be placed on a Control Roster.

Role of Defense Counsel

The role of the ADC tends to be much greater when discipline is handled by the squadron commander versus the supervisor. While ADCs are still only informed of administrative actions if airmen reach out to them, it was noted in our interviews that squadron commanders will often encourage their members to reach out to the ADC when they begin the administrative action process. This direction is likely in part because an administrative action issued by a commander is considered a more serious action than an administrative action issued by a supervisor. With an Article 15, when the commander begins filling out the form to let the airman know an Article 15 is being considered, the airman is automatically signed up for an appointment with the ADC's office. If the airman does not want the services of the ADC, they will need to actively cancel the appointment. It was noted in our interviews that airmen keep these appointments more than 90 percent of the time.

With both administrative actions and Article 15s, it is common for ADCs to help airmen craft a written response. The response often focuses on expressing contrition or noting extenuating circumstances, such as current difficulties in the airman's life. When an Article 15 has been initiated, the response may also note the hardship that various punishments might have on the airman. In particular, a rank reduction can be more detrimental for individuals if it happens when it is close to when they would time out of a promotion, so they might want to make the commander aware of this possibility.

Impacts on Airmen

The stakes of receiving disciplinary action by a squadron commander can be substantially higher than those of receiving discipline from a supervisor. While both authorities can issue an administrative action, it is considered to be a more serious mark on one's record when the commander issues it. Furthermore, as described above, a squadron commander has more tools to give the administrative action a bigger negative impact, as they can place the action into a UIF and place the member on a Control Roster. An Article 15 carries even more negative stigma, is almost certain to result in a UIF and Control Roster, and can result in serious punitive actions.

Whether the individual can recover from disciplinary actions at this stage and go on to have a successful career depends on the situation and how serious the disposition is. Receiving an Article 15 is considered an extremely serious disposition and would make it exceedingly difficult for an enlisted individual to ever make senior ranks. A key exception to this might be for individuals with otherwise exceptional records who have a one-time serious incident (such as a DUI) that merits either an LOR or an Article 15: These individuals might be able to recover, so long as the action does not occur at the time they are up for promotion. Many individuals receiving punishment at this stage have already received a lot of disciplinary actions at the supervisor stage; to the extent they get in repeated trouble at this stage (i.e., multiple LORs by the squadron commander and then an Article 15), they might face the prospect of an administrative discharge or be passed over for reenlistment. Finally, for certain offenses, such as marijuana use, there is a policy to pursue administrative discharge after a disciplinary action is taken (DAF IG, 2020).

Adjudication Process for Charges Preferred to a Court-Martial

If the squadron commander decides the case should be adjudicated through a court-martial, they will prefer the alleged charges to the court-martial convening authority, along with a summary of the evidence relating to each offense, information on prior disciplinary action taken against the airman, and a summary of the airman's service record (DoD, 2019). The squadron commander usually will submit this information to their wing commander, who has the authority to convene a summary or special court-martial. If the wing commander determines the case needs to be handled in a general court-martial, which typically handles the most-serious cases, the wing commander will prefer these charges to a senior commander who has the authority to convene a general court-martial. This senior commander is typically a general who is the commander of the numbered air force in the wing commander's chain of command. Throughout this section, we refer to these commanders as the court-martial convening authorities. Figure A.3 lays out the various activities that will occur once the convening authority receives the case. We discuss each of these stages in more detail below.

FIGURE A.3
Flow Chart of Court-Martial Process

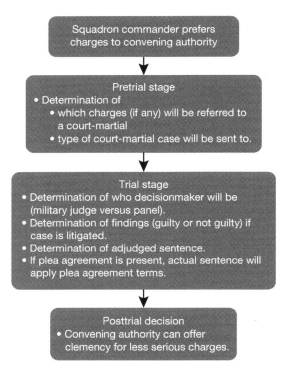

Pretrial Stage

Once receiving the case, the convening authority can decide that a court-martial should be convened, or they can elect to have the case be dismissed or handled through a less serious adjudicatory process, such as an Article 15 (Roan and Buxton, 2002). To convene a court-martial, there must be probable cause for each charge that will be referred there (DoD, 2019). For cases that are going to a general court-martial, this probable cause determination must be made through an Article 32 hearing (DoD, 2019), whereby a neutral officer (typically in the Judge Advocate General's Corps) oversees a probable cause hearing that both the prosecution and defense attorney participate in. For cases going to a summary or special court-martial, the probable cause determination can be made directly by the convening authority. During this stage, when probable cause is being assessed, the initial set of preferred charges can be changed. The final set of charges that will be adjudicated in a court-martial are the *referred* charges.

Simultaneous to the determination of the set of referred charges, the convening authority will determine the type of court-martial the case will be tried in (Roan and Buxton, 2002). A summary court-martial can only issue a maximum confinement sentence of 30 days, a special court-martial can issue up to a one-year sentence, and a general court-martial can sentence to the maximum penalty allowed under the UCMJ (DoD, 2019). Only enlisted individuals can be tried in a summary court-martial (DoD, 2019). A summary court-martial conviction is not considered a criminal conviction, whereas special and general court-martial convictions are considered misdemeanor and felony convictions, respectively (Breen and Johnson, 2018). Generally, the statutory maximum punishment for the most serious charge against the accused will play a dominant role in determining which court the case is tried in. For example, serious offenses for which the UCMJ allows long confinement sentences will need to be sent to a general court-martial, as that is the only court-martial that can assign confinement sentences longer than one year.

Court-Martial Trial Procedure

Prior to the start of a special or general court-martial, the airman must decide whether they want their case adjudicated by a military judge or by a panel of fellow airmen. Panels in a special court-martial consist of four members, while eight members are required in a general court-martial (DoD, 2019). Enlisted airmen can request that one-third of their panel be composed of enlisted airmen (DoD, 2019). Otherwise, the panel will consist of all officers. Cases involving capital offenses must go to a panel and require 12 members (DoD, 2019).

The adjudication process across the court-martial types is quite different. A summary court-martial has a less formal process. The trial is not run by a military judge but by a hearing officer, who is typically either a member of the Judge Advocate General's Corps or a neutral commander. The prosecutor and defense attorney are present, but there are no formal rules regarding what evidence will and will not be allowed (Roan and Buxton, 2002).

The hearing officer makes the final adjudicatory decision in this setting (Jeanne M. Holm Center, 2015).

The process by which cases are handled in special and general courts-martial is similar to the civilian criminal court process, in which formal rules of what evidence can be admitted are followed and a military judge presides over the proceeding. Circuit trial counsel (i.e., prosecutors) and circuit defense counsel will make opening statements, examine and cross-examine witnesses, present evidence, and make final arguments (Roan and Buxton, 2002); the local SJA office and ADC can also perform these roles. Either the military judge or a panel of airmen will make the adjudicatory decision in this setting (depending on whom the airman requested).

If an airman decides they want a panel to be the decisionmaker in their case, the convening authority will select the initial pool of potential panel members (Roan and Buxton, 2002). The local SJA office often provides a list of individuals who are stationed on the base where the trial is occurring and are available to serve on a panel. The convening authority will then select the individuals they think are best qualified for court-martial duty based on their age, education, training, and experience (DoD, 2019). Once this initial pool of panel members is determined, the selection procedure is similar to civilian jury trials, for which voir dire is conducted, and potential panel members can either be struck for cause or through the use of peremptory challenges by the prosecution and defense (Roan and Buxton, 2002).

There are two distinct decisions made during the court-martial. First, the hearing officer, military judge, or panel must decide whether the airman is not guilty, guilty of the charged offense, or guilty of a lesser included offense. If the airman is adjudged to be guilty, then the decisionmaker will also need to decide on the airman's sentence. If a panel is serving as the decisionmaker, a conviction occurs only if at least three-quarters of the panel members vote for a finding of guilty (DoD, 2019). Each offense has a statutory maximum for confinement that is listed within the UCMJ, and each court-martial type has a maximum confinement sentence the decisionmaker is allowed to issue. The confinement sentence the decisionmaker assigns must be at or below the minimum of these two thresholds (Roan and Buxton, 2002). In addition to confinement, the airman can receive a reprimand, a rank reduction, restriction, hard labor, pay forfeiture, a fine, a punitive discharge, and (in rare cases) the death penalty.

It is relatively common for the convening authority to work out a plea agreement with the airman prior to the start of the court-martial (Breen and Johnson, 2018). Often, plea discussions begin between the prosecutor and defense attorney, although the convening authority must approve all plea agreements. Typically, the deal will lay out the type of court-martial that will hear the case, the charges the airman will plead guilty to, and the maximum sentence that can be assigned. If the case is tried in a special or general court-martial, the airman will then need to determine whether they want a military judge or a panel to sentence them, and the trial will consist only of the sentencing phase. The military judge or panel is typically not aware of the maximum sentence that has been agreed to in the plea. The sentence the military judge or panel hands down is referred to as the *adjudged sentence* (Breen and Johnson, 2018). The airman's *actual sentence* is the minimum of the adjudged sentence and the sentence outlined in their plea agreement. Thus, the plea agreement effectively acts as a sentencing cap (Breen and Johnson, 2018).[2]

Posttrial Decisions

Once the actual sentence has been determined through the trial process, the convening authority can review the decision before the sentence becomes final. The convening authority cannot change a finding of not guilty to guilty or increase any of the punishments levied (Roan and Buxton, 2002). However, historically, Article 60 of the UCMJ gave the convening authority substantial discretion in setting aside findings of guilt or reducing the charge, as well as the power to commute or suspend the sentence (Weaver, 2020). This clemency power was not used often: Breen and Johnson (2018) find that, for court-martial convictions that occurred from 2005 to 2008, only 2 percent of cases received a form of clemency that resulted in a reduction in sentence severity. In 2013, these clemency powers were significantly curtailed by Congress: Now, the convening authority can downgrade guilt

---

[2] This policy changed for offenses that were committed on or after January 1, 2019, such that the sentencing authority (military judge or panel) is now informed of both the maximum and minimum sentence in the plea agreement. Thus, for offenses that occurred on or after January 1, 2019, the adjudged sentence is the same as the actual sentence. However, most of the data used in this study were subject to the prior policy.

findings or sentences only in cases that involve less serious offenses, which are defined as those for which the maximum punishment listed in the UCMJ is two years or less of confinement and for which the actual sentence assigned was six months or less (Weaver, 2020).

Impacts on Airmen

Receiving a court-martial conviction is likely to have lifelong consequences for an airman. First, as documented in Figure 4.3, more than 80 percent of convicted airman will receive a confinement sentence, and more than 35 percent will be punitively discharged from the DAF. Those who are convicted but are not punitively discharged are likely to face an administrative discharge hearing after their court-martial; a sexual assault conviction will result in an automatic discharge. Thus, once confinement sentences have been served, it is likely that the majority of these individuals will no longer be serving in the DAF. Furthermore, those convicted in a special or general court-martial will have a federal conviction on their record, which can make it difficult to find civilian employment.

Supplemental Material for Chapter 3

This appendix provides more detail about the construction of the dataset we used for the analyses presented in Chapter 3. We also provide more detail about the specifications we used to estimate the key results presented in Chapter 3. Finally, we examine how the main results shown in Figure 3.3 change when they are run on different subsamples, as well as when additional covariates (that are only available for part of the sample) are added. We also present results that show that the main conclusions from Chapter 3 do not change when Article 15s and court-martial referrals are treated as separate outcomes, rather than as one combined outcome.

Data Construction

In Chapter 3, we provided an overview of how we combined the AFPC data with the AMJAMS personnel data to construct our analysis sample. Here, we provide further detail on the sample drops made and on how some of the variables were constructed. For each fiscal year from 2010 through 2019, our initial sample included all enlisted individuals that were on active duty that year. These AFPC data were set up as a panel, such that individuals who served in multiple fiscal years during that period have a separate observation for each fiscal year of service. For a given fiscal year, the characteristics of these airmen were measured at the end of the previous fiscal year. This structure necessitated dropping 179,082 observations, which correspond to individuals in their first year of service, as characteristic information is not available for these airmen during the previous fiscal year. We then merged AMJAMS data into the AFPC data by Social Security number to identify which fiscal years (if any) these airmen were either issued an Article 15 or referred to a court-martial.

Airman race was identified through the AFPC data, which provided information on race and ethnicity. To develop mutually exclusive categories that combined race and ethnicity, individuals were assigned to categories in the following priority: Hispanic, Black, Native American/Alaska Native, Hawaiian Native/Pacific Islander, Asian, and White. We coded individuals who identified as multiracial or whose identified race/ethnicity changed over time as the first category in the ranking structure that was ever applicable to them. For example, if an airman ever identified as being Hispanic, regardless of what was listed in the race category, they were classified as Hispanic. If an individual identified as being both Black and Native American, they were coded as Black. We dropped 28,007 observations for which race was coded as either other or unknown. This left us with a total of 2,452,169 observations, which we used to construct Table 3.1. We used the subsamples of this larger sample that are noted in Figures 3.1 and 3.2 to construct those figures. Note that 26 observations were dropped between Table 3.1 and Figure 3.1 because rank was missing for these airmen.

All of the airman characteristics that we used to explain the racial disparity in discipline rates were obtained from AFPC data. The majority of these characteristics are listed in Table 3.2, although the analyses in Chapter 3 also included the location and occupation of the airman. Below, we discuss the construction of the variables that are not self-explanatory.

Home of record ZIP code characteristics were obtained by matching ZIP code characteristics to the ZIP code the airman resided in at the time they applied to the DAF. ZIP code characteristics were based on the 2010–2014 and 2015–2019 U.S. Census files; the values we used for each characteristic represented the weighted average for that characteristic across both files.[1]

With respect to the prior trouble variables listed in Table 3.2, the AFPC data have direct measures of whether an individual had a referral EPR or had an UIF opened. The AFPC data do not directly identify whether an airman had a previous incidence of being on a Control Roster or had a previous Article 15 or court-martial. However, the AFPC data indicate whether

---

[1]   We obtained the U.S. Census data from Manson et al., 2022.

one of these issues resulted in the individual either not being available for assignment or deployment or not being eligible for reenlistment. We thus coded individuals as having a previous Article 15 if they had ever had a previous instance of not being available for assignment or deployment, or were not eligible for reenlistment, because of an Article 15.[2] We constructed similar measures for both Control Rosters and courts-martial. Although these measures cannot identify previous incidents perfectly, they should do a reasonable job, as these incidents will usually restrict an airman's eligibility and availability for assignment. We could not use AMJAMS data to build prior records of Article 15s and courts-martial because we had only those data from 2010 to 2019. For an individual serving in 2010, the only way to get a thorough measure of their previous discipline history is by using the AFPC proxy measures.

To calculate the distance between the airman's current base and their home of record, we converted the ZIP codes available in the AFPC data into latitude and longitude coordinates.[3] We then applied the haversine formula to identify the distance in miles between the two ZIP codes.

To determine whether marijuana was legal in the state the airman lived in, we identified the year when marijuana was legalized for recreational use in each state (if ever). This information was obtained from data collected by RAND researchers as part of other projects involving the legalization of marijuana. From 2010 through 2019, 11 states legalized the recreational use of marijuana. For each person–fiscal year observation, we coded marijuana as being legal if the state where the airman lived allowed recreational marijuana use at the beginning of that fiscal year.

---

[2] This variable was lagged, such that when trying to explain whether someone had a disciplinary incident in fiscal year 2018 (measured by AMJAMS), the predictor variable is whether they had ever had a previous Article 15 up through the end of fiscal year 2016 (measured by AFPC data). The other predictor variables included would all have been measured at the end of fiscal year 2017. The reason why we lagged this variable by an additional year is that otherwise this indicator would have a strong probability of picking up the actual incident that occurred in 2018. For example, an airman who has a court-martial that ends in 2018 was likely already placed on restriction in 2017.

[3] We obtained a file from the National Bureau of Economic Research's (NBER's) website that listed the latitude and longitude coordinates for each ZIP code (NBER, undated).

To identify the population size of the surrounding counties, we first had to identify the county of the airman's current base and the surrounding counties (which are defined as *all adjacent counties*). The NBER provides a data file that identifies the surrounding counties of a given county (which includes the focal county as well).[4] We then merged in census data using the 2010–2014 and 2015–2019 files to provide information on the population size of the surrounding counties over this period.[5] We averaged the measures across the two census files, and thus each base has only one measure of population size for the surrounding counties over this period.

Airman occupation was coded using the first two values of the AFSC, which resulted in 37 categories.

Several of the variables were not available for everyone in the sample. About 3 percent of the male E1–E4 sample were missing either home of record ZIP code (from which several variables were derived) or AFQT percentile scores. While AFQT percentile scores seemed to be missing somewhat at random, ZIP code was not available for airmen with an accession date before fiscal year 2004 or for airmen who were not living in the United States at the time they entered the DAF. All variables based on AFQT scores and ZIP code are coded up in categorical form and include a category for a missing value; this allows us to not have to drop any observations because they are missing data on these characteristics.

Finally, the variable identifying whether the airman had a waiver was available only for those who entered the DAF in 2010 or later, and the variables coding the state legality of marijuana and the population size of the surrounding counties were available only for airmen who were residing in the United States. Because these variables were missing for such a significant portion of individuals and there was a systematic reason for these missing data, coding up a missing category for these individuals would not have produced relevant results, as the "missing" category would actually be picking

---

[4] The file obtained from the NBER can be accessed at NBER, 2017. To merge our data with this NBER data, we first needed to convert the ZIP code of the airman's base (available in AFPC data) into a Federal Information Processing Standard (FIPS) code. We obtained a crosswalk file from the U.S. Department of Housing and Urban Development, which we used to convert ZIP codes into FIPS codes (see U.S. Department of Housing and Urban Development, undated).

[5] These data are available from Manson et al., 2022.

up the impact of another variable. We thus decided not to use these controls in our main analysis so that we would not need to drop observations. However, we conducted robustness checks to examine the impact these variables had for the subset of observations for which this information is observed. These results are presented at the end of this appendix.

Model Specifications

In this section, we provide more detail on the specifications used to estimate several figures in Chapter 3.

Figure 3.3

To estimate Figure 3.3, we used the male E1–E4 subsample of the initial sample used for Table 3.1 (described at the beginning of this appendix); this subsample consisted of 888,879 observations. To identify the initial racial disparity in discipline rates when no controls are accounted for, we estimated the following model using ordinary least squares:

$$Discipline_{it} = \beta_0 + \beta_1 \times Black_i + \beta_2 \times Hispanic_i + \beta_3 \times Asian_i +$$
$$\beta_4 \times Hawaiian/Pac.Islander_i + \beta_5 \times American\ Indian/Alaskan_i + \varepsilon_i \tag{B.1}$$

Discipline is an indicator variable for whether airman i was either issued an Article 15 or referred to a court-martial in fiscal year t. The constant β_0 reflects the rate at which White airmen are either issued an Article 15 or referred to a court-martial, which is represented by the blue bar in Figure 3.3. $\beta_0 + \beta_1$ reflects the corresponding rate for Black airmen, and thus β_1 corresponds to the combined height of the orange and gray bars for Black airmen: i.e., the amount by which the rate for Black airmen exceeds that of White airmen. The other coefficients can be interpreted similarly, although we do not show the values for Asian and Native Hawaiian/Pacific Islander airmen in the figure, because these groups are disciplined at a rate that is lower than that of White airmen. Standard errors are clustered at the airman level.

To determine the part of the disparity that can be explained by airman characteristics, we now add controls into the model:

$$Discipline_{it} = \beta_0 + \beta_1 \times Black_i + \beta_2 \times Hispanic_i + \beta_3 \times Asian_i +$$
$$\beta_4 \times Hawaiian/Pac.Islander_i + \beta_5 \times American\ Indian/Alaskan_i + \quad \text{(B.2)}$$
$$\beta_6 \times Off\_Proxy_{it} + \beta_7 \times Occupation_{it} + \beta_8 \times Base_{it} + \beta_9 \times Year_{it} + \varepsilon_i$$

Off_Proxy includes controls for all variables listed in Table 3.2, with the exception of waiver status, state legality of marijuana, and the population size of the surrounding counties. (Including these variables would have required significant sample drops, as noted earlier. Robustness specifications are provided at the end of this appendix that include these controls and run the analysis on the subsample for which these variables are observed.) Equation B.2 also includes controls for the airman's occupation code, the base they were located at in a given year, and the fiscal year of the observation. Note that all the controls added in Equation B.2 have a *t* subscript, reflecting the fact that the values for these characteristics can change over time for a given airman. The coefficient β_1 in Equation B.2 reflects the disparity between Black and White airmen that remains once the covariates are controlled for. The percentage of the initial disparity between Black and White airmen that is explained by the included covariates can thus be measured as the percentage decrease in the β_1 coefficient from Equation B.1 to Equation B.2. We estimate this to be 20.2 percent, which corresponds to the height of the orange bar for Black airmen in Figure 3.3; the unexplained portion of the disparity is thus 79.8 percent, which is represented by the gray bar. We conducted a similar estimation for both Hispanic and American Indian/Alaska Native airmen.[6]

Figure 3.4

To estimate Figure 3.4, we conducted a Oaxaca-Blinder decomposition (Oaxaca, 1973; Blinder, 1973) on only the Black and White airmen who were included in the estimation for Figure 3.3 (which resulted in a sample size of 681,638). This decomposition is a regression-based technique that divides

---

[6] For Black airmen, the estimate of the unexplained disparity is similar to what we would have obtained if we had used a Oaxaca-Blinder decomposition. However, we did not use this decomposition method to construct Figure 3.3 because the decomposition method (as described in the discussion of Figure 3.4) requires estimating regressions separately by race. Because the number of American Indian/Alaska Native airmen is relatively small, we preferred to use the methodology described in this section.

the racial disparity in Article 15 and court-martial referral rates between Black and White airmen into an explained and unexplained portion (Jann, 2008):

$$\overline{Discipline_B} - \overline{Discipline_W} = (\overline{X_B} - \overline{X_W})\beta_W + \overline{X_B}(\beta_B - \beta_W) \qquad (B.3)$$

$\overline{X_B}$ and $\overline{X_W}$ represent the average values of non-race covariates included in Equation B.2 for Black and White airmen, respectively, and β_B and β_W represent the coefficients one would obtain on those covariates if Equation B.2 was run separately for Black and White airmen. The first term in Equation B.3 represents the explained portion of the disparity, as it reflects the proportion of the gap that results from Black and White airmen having different characteristics. Specifically, this term identifies how much higher Article 15s and court-martial referrals would have been for White airmen if they had had the same characteristics (on average) as Black airmen. The second term in Equation B.3 represents the unexplained portion of the disparity, as it represents how much of the gap results from a differential return on the same set of characteristics. For each characteristic included in Equation B.3, we then divided the value of the first term for that covariate by the overall disparity between Black and White airmen. Figure 3.4 displays the percentages for all covariates included that had at least some explanatory power for the disparity.[7]

Results for Other Subsamples

The majority of the estimation in Chapter 3 uses the male E1–E4 subsample, because that is the group that presents the highest likelihood of being issued an Article 15 or referred to a court-martial, and the disparity is the highest among this group. In Table B.1, we present the results from the specification used in Figure 3.3 in table form for several other subsamples. The first column corresponds to the male E1–E4 subsample, and thus the results are exactly as they were shown in Figure 3.3. In columns 2 and 3, we show the

---

[7]   The Oaxaca-Blinder decomposition was run using a logit specification. Standard errors were clustered at the airman level.

TABLE B.1

Percentage of the Racial Disparity That Is Unexplained for Various Subsamples of Enlisted Airmen

	Males Rank E1–E4	Females Rank E1–E4	Rank E5–E9	Specific Year for Male E1–E4 Sample		
				2010	2015	2019
Black	79.8%	79.5%	89.0%	68.2%	83.7%	83.0%
Hispanic	80.6%	50.8%	96.2%	60.9%	55.3%	80.7%
American Indian/ Alaska Native	91.3%	64.5%	80.3%	92.9%	85.2%	92.2%
Observations	888,879	211,687	1,351,577	86,601	87,879	86,837

NOTE: The percentages in the table correspond to the percentage of the racial disparity between that racial group and White airmen that is unexplained by the covariates controlled for. Each column represents a different subsample.

percentage of the disparity that is unexplained for the female E1–E4 sample and the E5–E9 (male and female) sample, respectively. The last three columns show the estimation for our preferred subsample using only one year of data at a time. We ran this specification to examine whether the panel data structure, in which a given airman was represented multiple times, affected our findings. Collectively, the results indicate that, regardless of the sample considered, the majority of the disparity is unexplained by any of the covariates we are able to control for.

Results Including Additional Covariates

None of the specifications presented up to this point have included controls for waiver status, state legality of marijuana, or population size of surrounding counties, as those variables were missing for a significant portion of our sample. In Figure B.1, we present the results of Oaxaca-Blinder decompositions for these three variables; these decompositions were run on smaller subsamples for which these variables were nonmissing. Specifically, to estimate the impact that waiver status has on the racial disparity in referral status, we reestimated Figure 3.4 using only the observations for which waiver status was nonmissing, which restricts the sample to those who entered the DAF in 2010 or later. We added waiver status into the model as an additional covariate; Figure B.1 is just presenting the results for that additional covariate, although we continue to include all previous variables in our model. Because the coefficient on waiver status is negative in Figure B.1, this indicates that the racial disparity in referral rates would actually increase by 0.2 percent if Black and White airmen were equivalent with respect to this characteristic.

To determine how much the population size of surrounding counties and state legality of marijuana explain racial disparities in referral rates, we again reestimated Figure 3.4, but now using only the observations for which these two variables were nonmissing, which restricts the sample to those who were stationed at a base in the United States. The results in Figure B.1 indicate that neither population size nor state legality of marijuana explains a statistically significant amount of the racial disparity. Thus, collectively, the results from Figure B.1 indicate that none of these three additional covariates explain the racial disparity in Article 15 and court-martial referral rates.

FIGURE B.1

How Much of the Article 15 and Court-Martial Referral Disparity Between Black and White Airmen Rank E1–E4 Is Explained by Waiver Status, Population Size of Surrounding Counties, and State Legality of Marijuana?

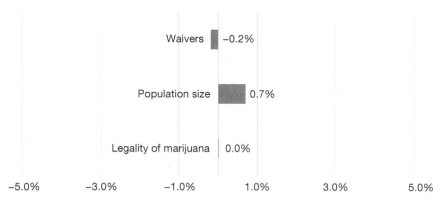

NOTE: Results were obtained using Oaxaca-Blinder decompositions. The impact of waivers was run on the sample used in Figure 3.4, where waiver status was nonmissing (n = 384,652). The impact of waiver status was statistically significant at the 5 percent level. The impact of population size and state legality of marijuana were run on the sample used in Figure 3.4 where these two variables were nonmissing (n = 567,525). The impact of each of these variables is statistically insignificant at the 10 percent level.

Results for Article 15s Versus Court-Martial Referrals

All the specifications in Chapter 3 combined the outcomes of being issued an Article 15 with being referred to a court-martial, as it was simpler to walk through the key results using one primary outcome. However, because being referred to a court-martial is more serious than being issued an Article 15, and because the latter occurs much more frequently, it is important to understand whether the main conclusions from Chapter 3 would have been different if these outcomes had been examined separately. The results in this appendix thus present the core results from Chapter 3 for the Article 15 and court-martial outcomes separately.

Figure B.2 presents the same information as shown for men in Figure 3.2, except separate comparisons of the racial disparity are shown for Article 15s

FIGURE B.2

Disparities in Article 15 Issuance and Court-Martial Referrals Among Rank E1–E4 Male Airmen

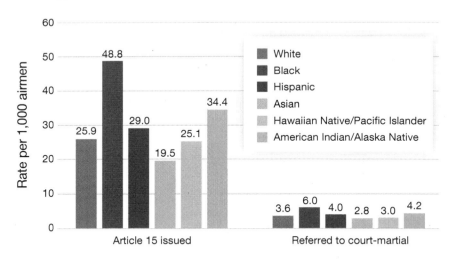

NOTE: This figure uses data on the male E1–E4 sample only. For the Article 15 outcome, with the exception of Hawaiian Native/Pacific Islander airmen, the disparities between each of the other race/ethnicities and White airmen are statistically significant at the 1 percent level. For the court-martial outcome, the difference between Black and White airmen is significant at the 1 percent level, the differences between Hispanic and Asian airmen and White airmen are significant at the 5 percent level, and the difference between Hawaiian Native/Pacific Islander and American Indian/Alaska Native airmen and White airmen is not significant.

and for courts-martial. The results indicate that, whether one examines the outcomes of Article 15s and courts-martial combined or separately, the key relationships are the same. Specifically, for both Article 15s and courts-martial, Black airmen are substantially more likely to receive these disciplinary outcomes than White airmen are, while the disparity between Hispanic and White airmen is much smaller.

Figures B.3 and B.4 present the same information as shown in Figure 3.3 but present the results separately for the Article 15 and court-martial outcomes. Figure B.3 shows how much of the disparity in Article 15 rates is explained by control variables that proxy for offending rates and controls for base, AFSC, and fiscal year. Figure B.4 presents these results for disparities in court-martial referrals. Note that we do not present results for American Indian/Alaska Native airmen in Figure B.4 because the results in Figure B.2 indicated the disparity between this group and White airmen was not sta-

FIGURE B.3

How Much of the Racial Disparity in Article 15 Rates Among Rank E1–E4 Male Airmen Is Unexplained?

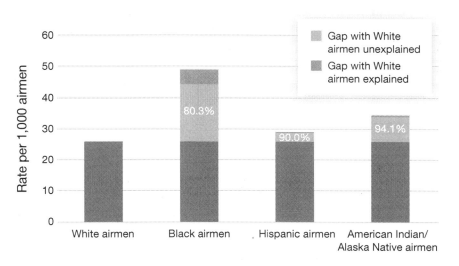

NOTE: This figure uses data on the male E1–E4 sample only (n = 888,879). The unexplained gap represents the size of the racial disparity that remains once control variables that proxy for offending rates have been included, as well as controls for base, AFSC, and fiscal year.

FIGURE B.4

How Much of the Racial Disparity in Court-Martial Referral Rates Among Rank E1–E4 Male Airmen Is Unexplained?

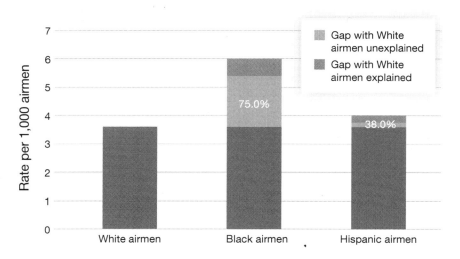

NOTE: This figure uses data on the male E1–E4 sample only (n = 888,879). The unexplained gap represents the size of the racial disparity that remains once control variables that proxy for offending rates have been included, as well as controls for base, AFSC, and fiscal year.

tistically significant. The results for Black airmen are similar regardless of the outcome examined.

Specifically, 80 percent of the disparity between Black and White airmen in the issuance of an Article 15 is unexplained by the control variables included, and 75 percent of the disparity between these two groups in court-martial referrals is unexplained. The results are somewhat different for Hispanic airmen, as almost all of the Article 15 disparity with White airmen is unexplained, whereas the majority of the court-martial disparity with White airmen is explained by the control variables included. However, the focus of our report was primarily on the disparity between Black and White airmen, as the disparities were much larger for Black airmen than for Hispanic airmen. Thus, the core conclusions in Chapter 3 remain unchanged.

Figures B.5 and B.6 present the same information shown in Figure 3.4 but present the results separately for the Article 15 and court-martial outcomes. Regardless of the outcome examined, the core results remain the

FIGURE B.5

How Much of the Article 15 Disparity Between Black and White Rank E1–E4 Male Airmen Is Explained by Individual Predictor Variables?

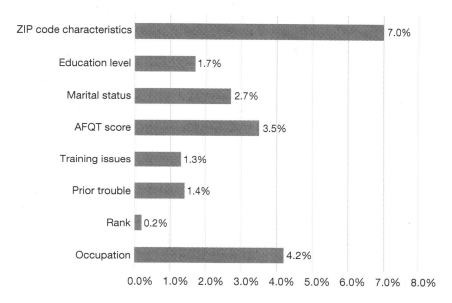

NOTE: Sample includes Black and White male airmen rank E1–E4, which consists of 681,638 observations. Results were obtained using Oaxaca-Blinder decompositions. With the exception of rank—which is significant at the 5 percent level—all variables presented in this table explain an amount of the disparity that is statistically significant at the 1 percent level.

same: The three factors that explain the largest amount of both the Article 15 and the court-martial disparity between Black and White airmen are home of record ZIP code characteristics, AFQT scores, and occupation.

Collectively, the results in this section indicate that combining Article 15 issuances and court-martial referrals into one outcome does not affect any of the core findings in Chapter 3.

FIGURE B.6

How Much of the Court-Martial Referral Disparity Between Black and White Rank E1–E4 Male Airmen Is Explained by Individual Predictor Variables?

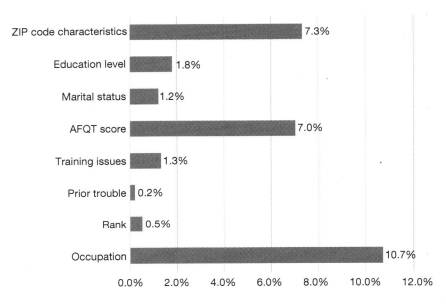

NOTE: Sample includes Black and White male airmen rank E1–E4, which consists of 681,638 observations. Results were obtained using Oaxaca-Blinder decompositions. Marital status, rank, and ZIP code characteristics do not explain a statistically significant amount of the racial disparity, while training is significant at the 5 percent level. The remaining variables are significant at the 1 percent level.

Supplemental Material for Chapter 4

This appendix provides more detail about the construction of the dataset used for the analyses presented in Chapter 4. We then provide evidence that our general findings presented in Chapter 4 are robust to controlling for case and airman characteristics and accounting for the adjudicatory pathways court-martial cases take.

Data Construction

The AMJAMS data extract we were provided included information on all airmen who were either issued an Article 15 or referred to a court-martial and had their case adjudicated in fiscal years 2010–2019. Because our project focused only on enlisted active-duty airmen, we dropped airmen who fall outside these categories. The AMJAMS data provided information on the full set of alleged offenses the airman was charged with, the outcome of the case (including sentence received), and characteristics of the airman, such as age, rank and specialty code, and the base where adjudication occurred. For cases referred to a court-martial, we observe whether the individual pled guilty to any of the charges, the type of court-martial the case was adjudicated in, and who the decisionmaker was. Note that while some subset of the individuals who pled guilty did so as part of a plea agreement, we do not observe which individuals had a plea agreement.

As discussed in Chapter 3, we also had personnel data on each of the airmen appearing in the AMJAMS data extract. Although the AMJAMS data provided information on the gender, race, and ethnicity of airmen, we instead chose to use the values that were present in the personnel data. While gender was almost equivalently coded in both datasets, there are clear differences in terms of how race and ethnicity are coded across these datasets (as noted in Appendix D), particularly with respect to Hispanic status. To keep these results consistent with our Chapter 3 results (for which we had to use race and ethnicity information from the personnel data), and because we feel the personnel race/ethnicity coding is more in line with official AFPC estimates, we continue to use the personnel classifications here.

We also used the information on previous trouble that was available in the personnel data. This information was described in detail in Chapter 3 and includes information on the presence of prior referral EPRs, UIFs, and Control Roster instances, as well as prior Article 15s and courts-martial. Note that while the personnel data likely do not provide a perfect measure of previous Article 15 and court-martial incidents, these data will cover everyone from the time they entered the DAF. In contrast, the AMJAMS data would provide this history only for events that were adjudicated in fiscal years 2010–2019.

To understand the extent to which the offenses an individual was charged with might explain the observed racial disparity, we needed to code up information on the severity and type of offense. For each of the most common offenses airmen were charged with, we used the maximum punishment chart from the UCMJ to code up the maximum period of confinement and pay forfeiture, as well as the type of punitive discharge allowed. For individuals charged with multiple offenses, we used these maximum punishments to identify the lead (most serious) offense. In our analysis, we measure the severity of the lead charge as the maximum allowed period of confinement and coded up the lead offense into the various types listed in Table 4.1. Because coding up the statutory maximums had to be done by hand and was relatively time-intensive, we did not code up offenses that occurred fewer than 20 times in the data. As discussed below, this decision resulted in a minimal sample drop.

The coding of the variables described above necessitated several sample drops of airmen who had missing values for these variables. Our initial sample of enlisted, active-duty airmen who were either issued an Article 15 or referred to a court-martial included 54,908 individuals. When merging in relevant personnel data on these individuals, we had to drop 889 airmen for whom we could not find a match in the personnel data. We then dropped an additional 3,339 observations for individuals for whom we did not code up their offense information. Further restricting the sample to male White, Black, and Hispanic airmen dropped an additional 9,046 individuals. This resulted in a total of 41,634 observations, which we used to estimate the summary statistics presented in Table 4.1.

The analyses examining racial differences in Article 15 punishments included only the 37,543 individuals who were issued an Article 15. As noted in Chapter 4, we examined racial differences on the part of the initial punishment that was not suspended. Thus, if an airman's initial punishment was a reprimand and a rank reduction, but the rank reduction was suspended, their punishment is coded as being a reprimand only. We could not identify the punishment for 459 airmen because of confusion in how the suspended sentence was coded, and thus these individuals had to be dropped from the analysis. Our remaining sample had 37,084 individuals; we used this sample to construct Figure 4.1.

The analyses examining racial differences in court-martial outcomes began by including the 4,091 individuals who were referred to a court-martial. We dropped 33 of these individuals because their sentencing outcome indicated that no trial was ever set. This left us with a remaining sample of 4,058, which we used to construct Figure 4.2. Figures 4.3 and 4.4 were created with the 3,465 individuals who were convicted of at least one charge in the process.

Robustness of Central Results

Our results in Chapter 4 indicated two key findings: (1) There were no racial differences in the Article 15 punishments issued, and (2) Black airmen do significantly better than White airmen in the court-martial process. In this section, we examine whether these conclusions are robust to including controls for case and airman characteristics, as well as the particular adjudicatory pathway the case takes in the court-martial process.

Robustness to Controlling for Case and Airman Characteristics

For simplicity, our results in Chapter 4 directly compared punishment outcomes across racial groups without controlling for the airman and case characteristics detailed in Table 4.1. Table C.1 examines whether our core conclusions change appreciably when these controls are included. For each outcome considered in the table, the first "no controls" row shows the comparison when no controls are included; these correspond to the results shown in Chapter 4. The second "controls" row presents the regression-adjusted comparisons, for which we regress (using ordinary least squares) the outcome variable on indicators for whether the airman is Black or Hispanic; controls for the age, rank, occupation, and previous trouble the airman has had; the maximum confinement and crime type of their lead charge; the number of offense types they were charged with; base; and the year their case was adjudicated. Because this controls row highlights the comparison, the baseline value for White airmen (which is just the average value of the outcome for this group) will not change. To obtain the regression-adjusted value for Black airmen, we sum the regression coefficient on the indicator for Black airmen with the baseline value for White airmen. This ensures that, when comparing the values for Black and White airmen, we are seeing the regression-adjusted difference. We constructed the values for Hispanic airmen in a similar manner.

The results in panel B of Table C.1 examine racial differences in punishments received among those receiving an Article 15. The results indicate that controlling for underlying case and airman characteristics does not change our overall finding in Chapter 4 that there are no sizeable racial differences in Article 15 punishments received. Note that even though some of the outcomes for Black and Hispanic airmen are statistically different than for White airmen, the magnitudes of these differences are quite small.

The results in panels C and D of Table C.1 examine racial differences in court-martial outcomes. The results generally indicate that, when we control for airman and case characteristics, the racial gap between Black and White airmen narrows somewhat for the acquittal outcome, as well as the likelihood of receiving a punitive discharge conditional on a conviction.

The narrowing of the racial disparity between court-martial outcomes for Black and White airmen that happens when controls are included likely occurs because White airmen whose cases are referred to a court-martial are more likely to have observable case characteristics that cause them to have worse court-martial outcomes than Black airmen. The fact that the gap narrows, but does not close, indicates that White airmen might have

TABLE C.1

Racial Disparities in Article 15 Punishments and Court-Martial Outcomes Among Enlisted Male Airmen

	White Airmen	Black Airmen	Hispanic Airmen
A. Sample: All defendants issued an Article 15 or referred to a court-martial (n = 41,634)			
Outcome: Percentage of defendants referred to a court-martial			
No controls	9.8%	9.4%	10.4%
Controls	9.8%	9.2%**	10.6%***
B. Sample: All defendants issued an Article 15 (n = 37,084)			
Outcome: Percentage of defendants receiving either no punishment or a reprimand only			
No controls	8.7%	8.1%*	8.2%
Controls	8.7%	8.5%	8.4%
Outcome: Percentage of defendants sentenced to either a pay forfeiture or a rank reduction			
No controls	76.2%	76.8%	78.0%***
Controls	76.2%	76.1%	77.7%***
Outcome: Percentage of defendants who were sentenced to a rank reduction			
No controls	54.0%	57.7%***	56.1%***
Controls	54.0%	54.9%	54.8%

Table C.1—Continued

	White Airmen	Black Airmen	Hispanic Airmen
C. Sample: All defendants referred to a court-martial (n = 4,058)			
Outcome: Percentage of defendants for whom an acquittal on all charges was issued			
No controls	12.7%	18.2%***	15.9%**
Controls	12.7%	16.7%***	14.0%
D. Sample: All defendants convicted in a court-martial (n = 3,465)			
Outcome: Percentage of defendants who received either a bad conduct discharge, a dishonorable discharge, or a dismissal			
No controls	39.8%	35.9%*	35.8%*
Controls	39.8%	37.3%	36.3%*
Outcome: Percentage of defendants who received a sentence of confinement			
No controls	82.5%	81.6%	81.4%
Controls	82.5%	80.7%	81.0%
Outcome: Average sentence length (in months), for which nonconfinement sentences are coded as zero			
No controls	10.3 months	6.9 months**	10.1 months
Controls	10.3 months	6.6 months***	8.6 months

NOTE: Sample in panel A includes male White, Black, and Hispanic airmen who are rank E1–E9. Panels B–D stratify this sample further, as indicated in the table. The asterisks indicate that the outcome for Black and Hispanic airmen is significantly different from the outcome for White airmen at the 1 percent (***), 5 percent (**), or 10 percent (*) level.

more-serious cases (or stronger evidence against them) in ways that can be observed (e.g., through the regression controls, which are picking up potential case severity) and in ways that are unobserved (e.g., through evidence strength). However, whether White airmen do worse because they have worse observable variables than Black airmen or because they have worse unobservable variables does not really matter. What matters most in this situation is that they do worse, because this would not be expected if the unexplained disparity in Chapter 3 were due to racial differences in offending rates. For this reason, we believe the raw comparisons presented in Chapter 4 to be the most relevant set of results.

Robustness to the Adjudicatory Pathway in Court-Martial Cases

The adjudicatory process for cases referred to a court-martial can take many different paths: Airmen might plead guilty, cases can be sent to three types of court-martial, and cases can be decided by a variety of decisionmakers. For simplicity, our analysis in Chapter 4 essentially ignored these various pathways and just examined racial disparities in overall court-martial outcomes. In this section, we examine whether there are observable and verifiable events prior to the findings phase of a court-martial that may explain why Black airmen referred to a court-martial have better outcomes than White airmen, as well whether we are missing any other important findings by focusing only on overall racial differences in outcomes. In other words, we want to ensure that Black airmen doing better at the court-martial stage is not being caused by the adjudicatory pathway their cases take but is instead independent of this pathway.

Table C.2 shows the frequency with which various adjudicatory pathways are taken, as well as how these frequencies differ across racial groups. Panel A shows the percentage of cases for which the airman pled guilty, as well as the percentage that are sent to each type of court-martial. Panels B and C show which decisionmakers the airman selects in special court-martial and general court-martial, respectively. Decisionmaker selections are not shown for summary courts-martial, as a hearing officer must make the decision in those cases. The first column indicates that 66 percent of airmen pled guilty to at least one charge and that more than half of the

TABLE C.2

Racial Differences in Court-Martial Adjudication Pathways Among Enlisted Male Airmen

	Overall	White Airmen	Black Airmen	Hispanic Airmen
A. All court-martial cases				
Guilty plea	66.3%	68.4%	61.1%	66.4%
Summary court-martial	19.0%	17.1%	22.6%	20.4%
Special court-martial	52.1%	54.0%	48.6%	51.0%
General court-martial	28.8%	29.0%	28.8%	28.6%
B. Decisionmaker in special court-martial cases				
Military judge	53.9%	54.2%	55.1%	51.3%
Panel includes enlisted	11.3%	10.0%	15.0%	10.8%
Officer-only panel	34.8%	35.7%	29.9%	37.9%
C. Decisionmaker in general court-martial cases				
Military judge	46.7%	47.9%	42.1%	49.3%
Panel includes enlisted	29.4%	25.2%	35.9%	34.0%
Officer-only panel	23.9%	26.9%	22.1%	16.8%

NOTE: Sample in panel A includes male White, Black, and Hispanic airmen who are rank E1–E9 and were referred to a court-martial.

cases go to a special court-martial. Military judges are the selected decision-maker in about half the special and general courts-martial cases. Enlisted members are more likely to be requested as part of the panel in a general court-martial than a special court-martial. Comparing the results between Black and White airmen indicates that Black airmen are less likely to plead guilty, more likely to have their case adjudicated through a summary court-martial, and more likely to opt for a panel that includes enlisted airmen.

The results presented in the remainder of this section examine the racial disparities within these different adjudicatory pathways for the two main outcomes for which racial differences were observed: acquittal rates and the length of confinement an airman is sentenced to (conditional on conviction). It is important to note up front that these adjudicatory pathways are not chosen randomly but rather are likely chosen by both the convening authority and the airman depending on the case characteristics. For example, while Table C.2 indicates that Black airmen are less likely to plead guilty, that does not mean that the reason Black airmen are more likely to be acquitted overall is because they are less likely to plead guilty. It is important to keep these nuances in mind when interpreting the results.

Figure C.1 shows how the racial differences in acquittal rates vary across court-martial types. Because our results in Chapter 4 (Figure 4.2) included guilty pleas, we dropped all cases in which the airman pled guilty when constructing Figure C.1 to show how the results are different when we examine acquittal rates only in cases in which airmen did not plead guilty. Because

FIGURE C.1

Racial Disparities in Acquittal Rates Across Court-Martial Types Among Enlisted Male Airmen

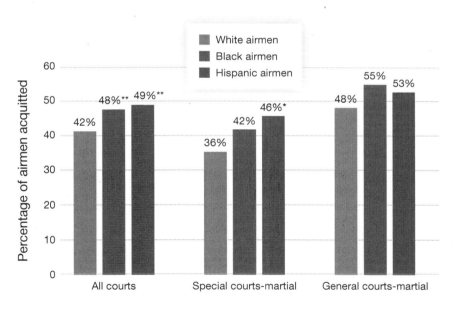

NOTE: Sample includes male White, Black, and Hispanic airmen who are rank E1–E9 and were referred to a court-martial but drops cases in which airmen pled guilty. The all courts sample included 1,327 observations, the special courts-martial sample included 617 observations, and the general courts-martial sample included 657 observations. There is no separate breakout for summary courts-martial because the number of cases that did not involve a guilty plea in those courts was too small. The asterisks indicate that the percentage for Black and Hispanic airmen is significantly different from the percentage for White airmen at the 1 percent (***), 5 percent (**), or 10 percent (*) level.

almost all the cases adjudicated in a summary court-martial involved a guilty plea, we examine racial differences in acquittal rates only in special and general courts-martial.[1] However, the summary court-martial cases that did not involve an airman pleading guilty are included in the "all courts" category. The results presented in Figure C.1 indicate that, even after dropping the cases in which airmen pled guilty, Black airmen are more likely to be acquitted, and this pattern is seen in both the special and the general courts-martial (although the racial differences for the special and general courts-martial are not statistically significant, likely because of the smaller sample size).

Figure C.2 shows how the pattern of acquittals varies across the types of decisionmakers airmen can select to adjudicate their case: a military judge, a panel of enlisted airmen and officers, or a panel that includes only officers. As in Figure C.1, we dropped cases in which airmen pled guilty, as decisionmakers are not making the acquittal decisions in these cases.[2] The results shown in Figure C.2 include cases tried in both special and general courts-martial. We do not include summary court-martial cases because only hearing officers handle those, so there is no comparison across decisionmakers to be made. The results indicate that all three groups of decisionmakers acquit Black airmen at a higher rate than White airmen.[3] Again, while none of the differences are statistically significant (likely because the subsamples we are working with are relatively small), the difference in magnitudes is consistent.

Figures C.3 and C.4 examine the other area in which Black airmen did significantly better than White airmen in the court-martial process: sentence lengths among those who were convicted. In Figure C.3, we show how the racial difference in sentence lengths varies across the three types of

---

[1]   The percentage of cases involving a guilty plea in summary, special, and general courts-martial was 93 percent, 70 percent, and 42 percent, respectively.

[2]   Eighty-four percent of cases handled by military judges in special and general courts-martial involved a guilty plea; these percentages were 15 percent and 46 percent for officer-enlisted panels and officer-only panels, respectively.

[3]   The acquittal rate comparisons between Hispanic and White airmen shown in Figures C.1 and C.2 are similar to what was shown in Figure 4.2: Specifically, Hispanic airmen are more likely to be acquitted than White airmen at the court-martial stage.

FIGURE C.2

Racial Disparities in Acquittal Rates Across Decisionmakers Among Enlisted Male Airmen

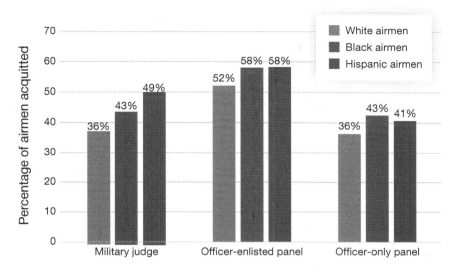

NOTE: Sample includes male White, Black, and Hispanic airmen who are rank E1–E9 and were referred to a court-martial but drops cases in which airmen pled guilty or that were tried in a summary court-martial. The military judge sample included 259 observations, the officer-enlisted panel sample included 483 observations, and the officer-only panel sample included 528 observations. The race/ethnicity groups denoted in the figure correspond to the accused airmen (not the decisionmakers). None of the percentages for Black and Hispanic airmen were statistically different than for White airmen at the 10 percent level.

courts-martial. The results indicate that the overall sentencing differences we see are really driven by what is happening in general courts-martial, as there are no racial differences present in summary or special courts-martial.

Figure C.4 shows how the racial difference in confinement sentences issued differs across decisionmakers. This figure includes only cases tried in a general court-martial, as Figure C.3 indicated that no racial disparities in sentence lengths were present in summary and special courts-martial. The results indicate that military judges, as well as panels that include both enlisted airmen and officers, assign lower sentences to Black airmen relative to White airmen. We find no racial differences in assigned sentences between Black and White airmen among the cases that are decided by officer-only panels. Note that our discussion of results here focuses on the

FIGURE C.3

Racial Disparities in Sentence Lengths Across Court-Martial Types Among Enlisted Male Airmen

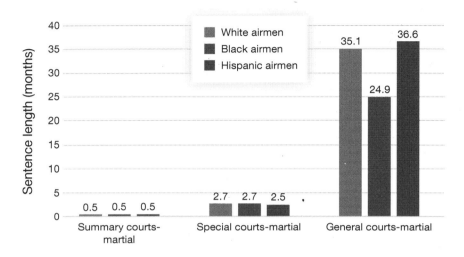

NOTE: Figure includes White, Black, and Hispanic male airmen rank E1–E9 who were convicted in a summary (n = 761), special (n = 1,876) or general (n = 828) court-martial, in which nonconfinement sentences are coded as a length of zero. None of the sentence lengths for Black and Hispanic airmen were statistically different than for White airmen at the 10 percent level.

magnitude of the difference in outcomes between Black and White airmen, as none of these differences are statistically significant (likely because of the small sample sizes).

Collectively, the results in this section support the assertion that Black airmen receive more favorable outcomes at trial than White airmen when we account for the adjudicatory pathway used. For the most part, the higher acquittal rates and lower sentences conditional on conviction are seen across courts and decisionmakers, and thus it does not seem to be the case that Black airmen have better outcomes because of the pathways their cases take.[4] The general finding that the average Black airman referred to a court-

---

4   An example whereby the court pathway might cause our acquittal findings would be if we found Black airmen to be much more likely to have their case sent to a general court-martial because they have a more serious case. As indicated in Figure C.1, acquittal rates are highest in a general court-martial, and thus having a dispropor-

FIGURE C.4

Racial Disparities in Sentence Lengths Across Decisionmakers Among Enlisted Male Airmen

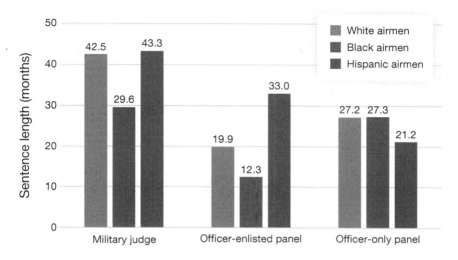

NOTE: Figure includes White, Black, and Hispanic male airmen rank E1–E9 who were convicted in a general court-martial. Military judge sample includes 456 observations, officer-enlisted panel sample includes 161 observations, and officer-only sample includes 206 observations. None of the sentence lengths for Black and Hispanic airmen were statistically different than for White airmen at the 10 percent level.

martial has better outcomes than the average White airman also seems to be present at both ends of the case severity distribution. At the lower end, Black airmen are more likely to have their case sent to a summary court-martial and have higher acquittal rates in special courts-martial. At the higher end, Black airmen have both higher acquittal rates and lower sentences in a general court-martial.

tionate number of cases going to a general court-martial likely would result in higher overall acquittal rates. This would then imply that Black airmen were more likely to be acquitted because they had more-serious cases that had to go to a general court-martial. However, the results in this section indicate this clearly is not happening. Table C.2 indicates Black and White airmen are equally likely to go to a general court-martial, and Figure C.1 indicates that, among the general courts-martial cases, Black airmen are more likely to be acquitted.

Race/Ethnicity Coding Across Datasets

Throughout this report, airmen race and ethnicity was obtained from the AFPC data. As mentioned in Chapter 3, there are some discrepancies between how the AFPC data and the AMJAMS data measure race and ethnicity, particularly with respect to identifying Hispanic airmen. In this appendix, we detail the differences between these two datasets in measuring race and ethnicity and discuss how this discrepancy can lead to some differences in the Article 15 and court-martial referral rates we report and in the rates detailed in the GAO (2019) and DAF IG (2021) reports.

Table D.1 identifies the differences between how the AFPC data and the AMJAMS data code race and ethnicity for the same sample. To obtain this sample, we began with the data used to construct Table 3.1, except we did not drop individuals who had an unknown (or value of other) for race and ethnicity. We then restricted the sample to those who either received an Article 15 or were referred to a court-martial, as this is the only set of individuals for which we observe race and ethnicity from AMJAMS and the AFPC. The resulting sample included 46,704 observations with race and ethnicity identifiers from both the AFPC data and the AMJAMS data. In Appendix B, we discussed how we constructed a mutually exclusive category that combined race and ethnicity for the AFPC data. We used this same coding scheme here with the AMJAMS race and ethnicity variables so that we could compare the datasets with respect to the combined race/ethnicity measure.

Table D.1 indicates that the biggest difference between the race/ethnicity measures in the two samples is with respect to how Hispanic airmen are

TABLE D.1

Comparing Race and Ethnicity Measures Between the AFPC and AMJAMS Data Among Enlisted Airmen

Race/Ethnicity	Percentage in AFPC Data	Percentage in AMJAMS Data
White	53.7	57.3
Black	24.5	25.1
Hispanic	15.7	9.6
Asian	2.3	2.5
Hawaiian Native/Pacific Islander	1.2	1.5
American Indian/Alaska Native	1.4	1.6
Other/unknown	1.2	2.4

NOTE: Sample includes 46,704 observations.

identified.[1] While the AFPC data indicate that Hispanic airmen make up 15.7 percent of airmen who receive disciplinary action, the AMJAMS data identify only 9.6 percent of this sample as being composed of Hispanic airmen. Comparing the results in the two columns indicates that many of the individuals who are identified as Hispanic in the AFPC data seem to be identified as other racial groups in the AMJAMS data, as the percentage of every other race/ethnicity group is higher in the AMJAMS data than in the AFPC data.

Because there are significant differences in how race/ethnicity is measured across datasets, it is important to discuss the effects this will have on how our reported Article 15 and court-martial referral rates compare with those reported in the DAF IG (2021) and GAO (2019) reports. The DAF IG report (2021) does not seem to have merged the AMJAMS and AFPC data but rather identifies the Article 15 and court-martial referral rate for a given race/ethnicity group by dividing the count of individuals issued an Article 15 or referred to a court-martial for that group (identified in the AMJAMS

---

[1] The race/ethnicity data in AMJAMS are input directly from AFPC's database using the accused's Social Security number. Table D.1 clearly indicates that the value input from the AFPC database seems to be different from what is in the AFPC database, although it is not clear what is driving this discrepancy.

data) by the full count of airmen in that race/ethnicity group (identified in the AFPC data). Because the AMJAMS data seem to be undercounting Hispanic airmen, this methodology results in a discipline rate for Hispanic airmen that is significantly lower than what we find: Although the numbers in the IG report indicate an Article 15 and court-martial referral rate of 13 for Hispanic individuals (in rates per 1,000 airmen), our results indicate a rate of 21.[2] As a result, while we find that Hispanic airmen are more likely to receive disciplinary action than White airmen, the results in the DAF IG report indicate the opposite. A similar issue arises for American Indian/ Alaska Native airmen in the DAF IG report. Although Table D.1 indicates the count of American Indian/Alaska Native airmen is only slightly higher in the AMJAMS data than it is in the AFPC data, any variation can make a big difference in discipline rates because the base population of this group is so small. As a result, although the results in the DAF IG report indicate that the discipline rate for this group is 39, we measure it as 23. This is why our results indicate the highest disparity is for Black airmen, whereas the DAF IG report measures American Indian/Alaska Native airmen as having the highest disparity.

The GAO report (2019) presents results only for White, Black, and Hispanic airmen and collapses all other individuals into either an other or an unknown category. By far, the most substantial difference between our results and GAO is with respect to the identification of Hispanic airmen. The stated methodology in the GAO report indicates that discipline rates were identified by merging the AFPC data with the AMJAMS data, which is the same methodology we use. However, GAO's estimates indicate that Hispanic airmen make up only 3 percent of both the airman sample and the discipline sample, whereas we find that Hispanic airmen make up 15 percent of the airman sample (Table 3.1) and 16 percent of the discipline sample (Table D.1).[3] Thus, although both studies used the AFPC data to identify

---

[2] This is the Article 15 and court-martial referral rate for all enlisted airmen, so it is not directly comparable to the rates presented in Figure 3.1. We obtained the Article 15 and court-martial referral rate estimates using the information presented in Figure 19 of the DAF IG (2021, p. 29) report.

[3] We obtained the GAO estimates of the proportion of Hispanic airmen from Tables 36 and 37 of the GAO report (2019, pp. 146–147).

race/ethnicity, the GAO report seems to be significantly undercounting Hispanic airmen. While we cannot definitively identify the reason for this difference, one potential reason is that the AFPC data includes two variables that measure ethnicity. The first variable corresponds to a yes or no question that asks airmen whether they are Hispanic or Latino. The second variable asks airmen more-detailed information about their ethnicity (e.g., whether they are Cuban, Latin American, Mexican, or Puerto Rican). It is not uncommon for airmen to select that they are Hispanic or Latino but then not answer the second ethnicity question. If we had identified Hispanic status using only the second variable, we would find that only 3.4 percent of the discipline sample consisted of Hispanic airmen, which is very similar to the GAO estimate. Thus, while we cannot definitively conclude that the GAO report used only one of the two Hispanic identifiers, this is potentially what happened.

Abbreviations

ADC	Area Defense Counsel
AFI	Air Force Instruction
AFPC	Air Force Personnel Center
AFQT	Armed Forces Qualification Test
AFSC	Air Force Specialty Code
AMJAMS	Automated Military Justice Analysis and Management System
DAF	Department of the Air Force
DoD	Department of Defense
DUI	driving under the influence
EPR	Enlisted Performance Report
GAO	Government Accountability Office
IG	Inspector General
LOA	Letter of Admonishment
LOC	Letter of Counseling
LOR	Letter of Reprimand
NBER	National Bureau of Economic Research
PIF	Personnel Information File
RIC	Record of Individual Counseling
SJA	Staff Judge Advocate
UCMJ	Uniform Code of Military Justice
UIF	Unfavorable Information File

References

AFI—*See* Air Force Instruction.

Air Force Instruction 36-2907, *Adverse Administrative Actions*, Department of the Air Force, May 22, 2020.

Air Force Instruction 51-202, *Nonjudicial Punishment*, Department of the Air Force, March 31, 2015.

Air Force Personnel Center, "Air Force Demographics," webpage, undated. As of February 14, 2023:
https://www.afpc.af.mil/The-Air-Forces-Personnel-Center/Demographics/

Air Force Personnel Center News Service, "Personnel Information Files No Longer Required," Andersen Air Force Base, January 8, 2008.

Alexander, Michelle, "The New Jim Crow," *Ohio State Journal of Criminal Law*, Vol. 9, No. 1, 2011.

Benartzi, Shlomo, Ehud Peleg, and Richard H. Thaler, "Choice Architecture and Retirement Savings Plans," in Eldar Shafir, ed., *The Behavioral Foundations of Public Policy*, Princeton University Press, 2013.

Blinder, Alan S., "Wage Discrimination: Reduced Form and Structural Estimates," *Journal of Human Resources*, Vol. 8, No. 4, Autumn 1973.

Breen, Patricia D., and Brian D. Johnson, "Military Justice: Case Processing and Sentencing Decisions in America's 'Other' Criminal Courts," *Justice Quarterly*, Vol. 35, No. 4, 2018.

Chetty, Raj, Nathaniel Hendren, and Lawrence F. Katz, "The Effects of Exposure to Better Neighborhoods on Children: New Evidence from the Moving to Opportunity Experiment," *American Economic Review*, Vol. 106, No. 4, April 2016.

Christensen, Don, and Yelena Tsilker, *Racial Disparities in Military Justice: Findings of Substantial and Persistent Racial Disparities Within the United States Military Justice System*, Protect Our Defenders, May 5, 2017.

DAF IG—*See* Department of the Air Force Inspector General.

Department of Defense, *Report of the Task Force on the Administration of Military Justice in the Armed Forces*, November 30, 1972.

Department of Defense, *Manual for Courts-Martial United States (2019 Edition)*, 2019.

Department of the Air Force Form 3070, "Record of Nonjudicial Punishment Proceedings," Department of the Air Force, undated.

Department of the Air Force Inspector General, *Report of Inquiry (S8918P): Independent Racial Disparity Review*, December 2020.

Department of the Air Force Inspector General, *Report of Inquiry (S8918P): Disparity Review*, September 2021.

Department of the Air Force Judge Advocate General, "Report of the Judge Advocate General of the United States Air Force: October 1, 2016 to September 30, 2017," 2017. As of July 20, 2023: https://www.armfor.uscourts.gov/annual/FY17AnnualReport.pdf

DoD—*See* Department of Defense.

Dunlap, Charles J., Jr., "Military Justice," in David M. Kennedy, ed., *The Modern American Military*, Oxford University Press, 2013.

Forscher, Patrick S., Calvin K. Lai, Jordan R. Axt, Charles R. Ebersole, Michelle Herman, Patricia G. Devine, and Brian A. Nosek, "A Meta-Analysis of Procedures to Change Implicit Measures," *Journal of Personality and Social Psychology*, Vol. 117, No. 3, 2019.

Goldin, Claudia, and Cecilia Rouse, "Orchestrating Impartiality: The Impact of 'Blind' Auditions on Female Musicians," *American Economic Review*, Vol. 90, No. 4, September 2000.

Government Accountability Office, *Military Justice: DOD and the Coast Guard Need to Improve Their Capabilities to Assess Racial and Gender Disparities*, GAO-19-344, May 2019.

Jeanne M. Holm Center, "Military Justice," in Jeanne M. Holm Center, Air and Space Studies 400: National Security Affairs/Preparation for Active Duty, 2015–2016 ed., 2015.

Jann, Ben, "The Blinder-Oaxaca Decomposition for Linear Regression Models," *Stata Journal*, Vol. 8, No. 4, December 2008.

Judge Advocate General's School, *The Military Commander and the Law*, 13th ed., 2016.

Judge Advocate General's School, *The Military Commander and the Law*, 18th ed., 2022.

Lochner, Lance, "Education and Crime," in Steve Bradley and Colin Green, eds., *The Economics of Education: A Comprehensive Overview*, 2nd ed., Elsevier, 2020.

Lochner, Lance, and Enrico Moretti, "The Effect of Education on Crime: Evidence from Prison Inmates, Arrests, and Self-Reports," *American Economic Review*, Vol. 94, No. 1, March 2004.

Manson, Steven, Jonathan Schroeder, David Van Riper, Tracy Kugler, and Steven Ruggles, "IPUMS National Historical Geographic Information System," version 17.0, IPUMS, 2022. As of July 31, 2023: https://www.nhgis.org

National Bureau of Economic Research, "Public Use Data Archive," webpage, undated. As of July 31, 2023: https://www.nber.org/research/data

National Bureau of Economic Research, "County Adjacency," webpage, updated May 8, 2017. As of July 31, 2023: https://www.nber.org/research/data/county-adjacency

National Gang Intelligence Center, *National Gang Report*, 2015.

NBER—*See* National Bureau of Economic Research.

Oaxaca, Ronald, "Male-Female Wage Differentials in Urban Labor Markets," *International Economic Review*, Vol. 14, No. 3, October 1973.

Pew Research Center, "The Military-Civilian Gap: Fewer Family Connections," November 23, 2011.

Quintanar, Sarah Marx, "Man vs. Machine: An Investigation of Speeding Ticket Disparities Based on Gender and Race," *Journal of Applied Economics*, Vol. 20, No. 1, May 2017.

Redbird, Beth, and Kat Albrecht, "Racial Disparity in Arrests Increased as Crime Rates Declined," Northwestern Institute for Policy Research, June 18, 2020.

Roan, James B., and Cynthia Buxton, "The American Military Justice System in the New Millennium," *Air Force Law Review*, Vol. 52, Winter 2002.

Robinson, Barry K., and Edgar Chen, "Déjà Vu All Over Again: Racial Disparity in the Military Justice System," Just Security, September 14, 2020.

Rothstein, Richard, *The Color of Law: A Forgotten History of How Our Government Segregated America*, Liveright Publishing, 2017.

Sabol, William J., Thaddeus L. Johnson, and Alexander Caccavale, *Trends in Correctional Control by Race and Sex*, Council on Criminal Justice, December 2019.

Sentencing Project, "Regarding Racial Disparities in the United States Criminal Justice System," March 2018.

Spohn, Cassia, "Race, Crime, and Punishment in the Twentieth and Twenty-First Centuries," *Crime and Justice*, Vol. 44, 2015.

Thomas, Pierre, John Kelly, and Tonya Simpson, "ABC New Analysis of Police Arrests Nationwide Reveals Stark Racial Disparity," ABC News, June 11, 2020.

U.S. Department of Housing and Urban Development, "HUD USPS ZIP Code Crosswalk Files," webpage, undated. As of July 31, 2023:
https://www.huduser.gov/portal/datasets/usps_crosswalk.html#codebook

Weaver, Jacob R., "Restoring the Power of the Convening Authority to Adjust Sentences," *Michigan Law Review*, Vol. 119, No. 3, 2020.

Worden, Robert E., Sarah J. McLean, Robin S. Engel, Hannah Cochran, Nicholas Corsaro, Danielle Reynolds, Cynthia J. Najdowski, and Gabrielle T. Isaza, *The Impacts of Implicit Bias Awareness Training in the NYPD*, John F. Finn Institute for Public Safety, July 2020.